LIGHT YOUR FIREBRAND

Re-igniting Your Business and Your Brand

Mike Symes

To Jayne

n A Firebrand in Your own right

Best Wishes

Mike Symes

Light Your Firebrand

First published in 2011

Ecademy Press

48 St Vincent Drive, St Albans, Hertfordshire, AL1 5SJ

info@ecademy-press.com www.ecademy-press.com

Printed and Bound by Lightning Source in the UK and USA

Cover Design: John Dillon

Typesetting by Charlotte Mouncey

Printed on acid-free paper from managed forests. This book is printed on demand, so no copies will be remaindered or pulped.

ISBN 978-1-907722-02-8

Acknowledgements

To all the brands that light me up. And for everyone who dares to gaze into the flames to see something new. This book is for you.

Contents

About the Author

Mike Symes is a multi-award winning branding strategist, communications expert, author and professional speaker.

The founder of the Strand group of companies (Strand Branding Limited and Strand Financial Limited), Mike has a passion for branding and communications, drawing on over 20 years top-level experience working with global financial services brands.

He is also Chairman of online publishing company, Financial Marketing Limited, and FIDES, the premier networking group of service providers to financial institutions.

Mike's senior client-side roles have included Brown Shipley, Credit Lyonnais, and Banque Paribas group and, latterly, Head of Marketing at Bank of New York Financial.

In 1998, Mike was granted the Freedom of the City of London, one of the oldest traditional ceremonies still in existence.

Fireword

"Branding is one of the hottest trends in business – and one of the most misunderstood."

Wall Street Journal

For billions of years, our planet has been in a constant state of seismic change. Generating. Destroying. Regenerating. Healing itself yet again in an endless pattern of self-renewal.

In recent years, we have seen news presenters from Wall Street to the Square Mile searing our senses with the rhetoric of 'flames rising inexorably to engulf our global financial system'. From IndyMac ("you can count on us") and Lehman Brothers ("where vision gets built") to Washington Mutual ("Whoo hoo") - whose slogan alone surely should have alerted investors to their appetite for risk - there have been numerous financial institutions consumed by the credit firestorm sweeping the globe.

A number of organizations have emerged with charred reputations. Some have survived with their reputations intact and a few have even thrived in this fragile new environment. Others have risen phoenix-like from the still smoking debris of the competitive landscape.

Today, the banking sector has begun to show tangible signs of recovery, with the world's 500 most valuable banking groups growing by 62% in terms of market capitalization and their brand values cumulatively increasing by 49%, according to the fourth edition of the BrandFinance® *Banking 500* – an annual review of the top banking brands in the world, published in conjunction with *The Banker*.

Re-establishing trust and confidence is fundamental to sustained business success, but is not in itself nearly enough to gain new ground or breakthrough results. In fact, for many organizations, complete ground-up re-invention is required. One thing is for sure. Out of the ashes of apparent destruction will emerge an entirely new world order. A new landscape you can make your own – your 'brandscape'.

However, worryingly, recent research has revealed that 70% of financial firms in the U.S. and the UK are not sufficiently differentiated from their competitors.

Today, most service based organizations and their marketing agencies seem intent on simply communicating stability. However, in the current climate, it is essential to traverse the vectors of both stability and change simultaneously.

Whilst a number of the examples featured in this book draw directly from my experience in the financial services sector, the 'learnings' can be applied equally to any industry. Branding is not purely the remit of large institutions with the luxury of vast budgets. The Internet has gone a long way to level the playing field. For the first time, small independent market entrants have an opportunity to sweep away the established sleeping giants. The giants (possibly) have a once in a lifetime opportunity to reboot themselves and go for radical re-invention.

When the future was an extension of the present, it was reasonable to assume that what worked today would also work next year. That assumption must now be cast aside. During times of change, it can almost be guaranteed that what used to work well in the past will not work at all next time around. The old approaches are at best simply too incremental at a time when success needs to be measured by growth that is exponential.

To achieve sustained success in today's challenging environment, the new imperative for all businesses is to fight fire with fire. It's time to Light Your Firebrand™.

Lighting Your Firebrand

"Surely I see fire; I will bring to you from it some news, or I will bring to you therefrom a burning firebrand so that you may warm yourselves."

Quran

Welcome to Basecamp

"I am irresistible, I say, as I put on my designer fragrance.
I am a merchant banker, I say, as I climb out of my BMW.
I am a juvenile lout, I say, as I pour an extra strong lager,
I am handsome, I say, as I put on my Levi jeans."

John Kay

Well done for taking the first step on your branding journey. You've got to Firebrand basecamp.

When I run a Light Your Firebrand™ Workshop, either with a management team or within a conference environment, I often start by asking what the participants have in mind when they think of the word, 'brand'. Generally, this prompts a variety of responses along the following lines:

- Corporate identity / logo
- Corporate image
- Bundle of values / benefits
- Trust
- Product

- Perception
- Promise
- Defines the business
- Corporate DNA
- Clear, consistent direction

And here's my personal favorite from one of my clients based in China, Wong Meng Choong, the managing director of Asian operations for DTF, who defines a brand more poetically as "the face and soul of an organization."

If you believe that a brand extends to a place far beyond a logo mark, then you'd be right. A Firebrand is to be found in an entirely different dimension. An individual one. A distinctly personal one. And increasingly, in this age of hyper-competition, an emotional one.

Re-igniting Your Business

Tinder-Spark-Flame-Glow

I have developed the 4Rs model, referred to throughout this book, to highlight the four distinct, and ideally balanced attributes that are shared by all world-class brands in the hearts and minds of their customers:

RELEVANT (TINDER)

The appropriateness of brand 'fit' to customer / stakeholder wants and needs.

REMARKABLE (SPARK)

The distinguishing nature / uniqueness of the brand in the context of customer perception.

REPUTATIONAL (FLAME)

The level of trust, respect and esteem gained by a relationship with the brand.

REAL (GLOW)

The degree of emotional involvement and depth of engagement with the brand.

This model is not only a powerful starting point to propel your business, it is the basis for managing your brand effectively and with greater clarity over the long term.

The 4Rs

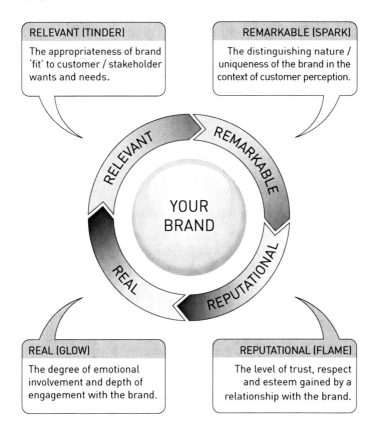

RELEVANT (TINDER)
The appropriateness of brand 'fit' to customer / stakeholder wants and needs.

REMARKABLE (SPARK)
The distinguishing nature / uniqueness of the brand in the context of customer perception.

YOUR
BRAND

RELEVANT

REMARKABLE

REAL

REPUTATIONAL

REAL (GLOW)
The degree of emotional involvement and depth of engagement with the brand.

REPUTATIONAL (FLAME)
The level of trust, respect and esteem gained by a relationship with the brand.

Reposition, revitalize or rebrand?

In addition to mergers or acquisitions, brand reposition-ing, revitalization or rebranding is essential when one or more of the following conditions exist:

Relevant (Tinder)

Your current positioning is no longer relevant or appro-priate to your market and has therefore stagnated or is confusing – or – you have found a way to re-invent your brand to keep pace with customer needs (e.g. services, accessibility, convenience, choice, style, technology).

Remarkable (Spark)

A differentiated benefit has become regarded as a cost-of-entry benefit – or – you have identified a powerful and specific advantage or opportunity to differentiate your brand.

Reputational (Flame)

A new competitor with a superior value proposition enters your industry – or – you have recognized an opportunity to leverage and extend your reputation and sphere of influence into new areas and industries.

Would Internet financial services brands Egg, Smile and Cahoot have captured the imagination quite as well had they stuck with the names of their parent companies Prudential, Cooperative Bank and the Abbey National?

Real (Glow)

Your brand has emerged from a crisis situation with a tarnished image – or – you have seen a way of aligning yourself with a cause that matters to people, creating a common sense of purpose and unified identity.

Accenture must be delighted to no longer bear the Andersen name in the wake of the Enron scandal that has severely damaged the reputation of the accountancy giant with which it was once associated.

My 4Rs moment

Please indulge me for a moment and excuse me if I get a little emotional. Let me tell you about my latest purchase - my stunningly beautiful Gibson Songwriter guitar.

What I was searching for was a guitar that was **relevant** to my needs, a high quality electro-acoustic guitar in cutaway style that offers great playability. One that I could play plugged or unplugged.

What I discovered when I visited the local music store was that most guitars in my chosen price segment looked and sounded much the same. But there was something missing in all of the guitars I tried – personality! That is, until I saw the object of my desire right at the back of the store. The quality of the hand-finished woods and pearl inlays caught my attention at first glance. And then, from the moment I actually picked up the guitar, the warmth and diversity of tone just blew me away. Here was a truly **remarkable** guitar that made for an unforgettable playing experience.

As for its **reputational** quality, it is a Gibson and consequently a 'no-one got fired for buying an IBM' style decision. It is a make of scintillating reputation, endorsed by many of the greatest guitarists and singer songwriters in the world. The feeling of ownership is a **real** and lasting pleasure, which makes me want to pick it up and play and continually feel rewarded and privileged for having done so. My beloved Gibson Songwriter – the total brand experience and the 4Rs in perfect balance.

What brand experiences light you up?

What is a Firebrand?

"He was raring to go ... He said he was ready to go out there and start being a firebrand again."

Russ Kinnel

This practical 'how-to' book offers you an insider's view as to what it means to create a Firebrand and how we have created billions of pounds of additional revenues and profits for our clients as a direct result of implementing the transformational branding process you see here.

A Firebrand ignites your compelling purpose, enabling you to develop an original big idea that burns more brightly than anyone in your market. It sparks the imaginations of your employees, customers and other stakeholders, turning them into torchbearers who love to share your big idea with others.

Your Firebrand will illuminate your company's irresistible points of difference, so your business shines out above the rest. With the firepower to dominate your chosen niche, your fresh, inspiring, evocative messages will spread like wildfire. Then, watch your profits soar skywards!

The results are best summed up by one of my clients / torchbearers: "I have now experienced Light Your Firebrand™ workshops for three of my businesses at different stages of development, from start-up to Royal Warrant holders. In an effective way, the workshop participants are challenged to re-consider their approach to selling and marketing their products and their business. In each case, the management of the business has left with a dramatically enhanced clarity of thought in respect of their business proposition. Whilst each business has extracted a range of specific benefits from the workshop, the common theme is that things will never be the same again."

You can create a Firebrand

- By defining a differentiated 'core essence' at the heart of your brand and your business.

- By reinventing your organization to deliver your unique value propositions in a relevant and remarkable way that meets the needs of your customers, prospects and partners.

- By building a heightened emotional connection with your clients at every level of engagement.

- By using measurable marketing techniques across multiple channels to generate enquiry, build awareness and encourage dialogue and referral.

So, what are you waiting for? Grab your torch and let's go.

Lighting Yourself Up

"Success is not the result of spontaneous combustion. You must first set yourself on fire."

Fred Shero

It was a dark afternoon at our first-ever marketing agency's offices, just before Christmas. One of those afternoons, where we had some time and space to think about the following year's objectives.

Several new business wins to 'bed down'. No account management issues outstanding. Some encouraging pitch activity for the New Year. Quite ordinary really. Rather, it would have been if I hadn't decided to inflict a strategic workshop on the team.

Our Creative Director, John Dillon, found the concept of an in-house workshop pretty amusing. Even funnier than that, actually. "How very corporate man that is!" came his spirited volley in my direction. "You really should have warned me." More laughter.

Now, I have put together strategy workshops of this kind many times before. Clients tell me that they have found them pivotal to their successful re-invention and revitalization.

To their credit, the team mustered a degree of enthusiasm for what I'm sure they saw as some form of navel intro-spection. Some nods of agreement on minor points fol-lowed as I rattled through the SWOT Analysis (strengths, weaknesses, opportunities, threats). So far, so good. Or so I thought.

Then came the crunch question. I asked the team to come up with 10 points of difference between our agency and other full service agencies. I wheeled out the traditional 'brand onion.' Skinned it. Presented it. Silence. Nothing. Numbness.

Then I looked over at John and I could see we both wanted to 'smash the onion.' Tear the thing apart. It was a Eureka moment. Energizing.

I now believe the result of this exercise was far more significant than any of us had recognized at the time - a turning point. It's just what the meeting had failed to tell us that was really important. I must have needed to go through that. Take the tough journey. I suspect that John had already reached that point. The conversation was mutually telepathic, something along the lines of Steve Jobs' mantra: "We're here to put a dent in the universe. Otherwise, why else even be here?"

The need to create market differentiation and distinction is a challenge that's not reserved purely for an agency's clients. The plethora of undifferentiated messages from generalist consultancies and agencies is evidence enough to support this claim and serves only to add to the noise and clutter echoing around the corporate landscape. You see, where we were at that time simply no longer lit us up. It didn't inspire or move us. We needed to change dramatically. To transform our clients' brands, we needed to first light our Firebrand.

Getting Off the Brandwagon

"We are each gifted in a unique and important way. It is our privilege and our adventure to discover our own special light."

Mary Dunbar

As I was walking on London's South Bank, I stopped to listen to a very talented busker. A line in the first verse of his song really struck a chord with me: "Indifference feels the same." It reminded me of a quote I read from Dan Clark: "In today's business environment, the word 'same' could be shorthand for 'out of business'."

The Swedish academics, Jonas Ridderstrale and Kjell Nortstrom sum up the situation perfectly: "The 'surplus society' has a surplus of similar companies, employing similar people, with similar educational backgrounds, working in similar jobs, coming up with similar ideas, producing similar things, with similar prices and similar quality."

In an example which is very close to home, a CEO of a large international bank told me that he 'could put a credit card' between his organization and his major competitors, the difference was so slim.

You see, it's all too easy to lose sight of 'who you are' as a business, particularly if it has evolved. As you take on new people, new clients, new channels, and particularly when you become involved in mergers and acquisitions, it is so often the case that the central spark that once lit up your business flickers and falters along the way.

Differentiate your differentiation strategy

Michael Porter tells us that, "We need to start moving into the next phase, which is one of strategy, the phase in which individual banks make choices about how they are going to be distinctive, how they're going to be unique, how they're going to set themselves apart."

However, scanning through the advertisements of financial organizations in trade magazines from both sides of the Atlantic on a flight to New York, I couldn't help but notice that most organizations are claiming exactly the SAME attributes as differentiators within their respective journals.

Statements such as: "What differentiates us is our people, service, flexibility and innovation," peppering journals, brochures and web sites seem to me to be having the opposite effect to what these companies intended.

To achieve long-term success in today's customer-driven marketplace, you first need to differentiate your differentiation strategy!

Ironically, it follows that the greater the organizational focus on these commonly held attribute areas, the more similar these companies must appear in the eyes of their potential customers.

Message mediocrity

I never cease to be amazed at the sheer volume of direct mail I receive from services organizations (I keep them all) and how very similar these pieces are.

Rather than being centered on a point of difference, all of the communications focus upon the well-travelled but unremarkable trail of product and service features and benefits:

1. Better rates
2. Higher returns
3. Personal service
4. Fast turnaround
5. Product specific benefits - including insurance, identity protection, travel benefits
6. Affinity programs - sport, holidays etc

The majority of these direct mail pieces feature happy families, happy employees and serious bankers. In other words, corporate wallpaper.

As Frank Capek observed: "The challenge is that most banks have a long legacy of product-centric, 'everything for everybody' ways of thinking. This leads to decision-making and resource commitments that reinforce 'better sameness' rather than true differentiation."

And that's the challenge that faces each and every one of us – the avoidance of corporate wallpaper; pleasant enough but ultimately unremarkable.

As Ann Livermore of Hewlett-Packard said: "These days, building the best server isn't enough. That's the price of entry."

Accidental positioning

The danger of not evolving your brand and ensuring its freshness and appeal is perhaps best explained by the Chinese proverb: "If you do not plan for the future, you will get the one that shows up".

So, the real danger is that if you don't create a clear position for your business, the market will create one for you. Accidental positioning is one of the most critical issues facing businesses today. The imperative is to ensure your brand doesn't happen by accident. The real opportunity to gain a competitive advantage is for you to focus and develop different attributes from your competitors and to build your customer experience from that solid foundation.

Short branding

The term, 'short selling' has dominated the press of late (although if, like me, you have been immersed in financial services marketing, I would forgive you for not wanting to dwell on the torrid headlines).

'Short selling' or 'shorting' is the practice of selling things that the seller does not own (in the hope of purchasing them later at a lower price).

It struck me that 'short branding' is the practice of promoting attributes that the seller does not own. The key to creating a Firebrand is to identify attributes that your competitors do not own.

Don't become benchmarked out!

W. Chan Kim and Rene Mauborgne wrote a challenging piece in the *Financial Times* entitled, "Think for yourself - stop copying a rival." They explained: "Companies need to break out of a vicious cycle of competitive benchmarking and imitation. Aiming to beat the competition has the opposite effect to the one intended. It keeps companies focused on the competition. When asked to build competitive advantages, managers typically rate themselves against competitors, assess what they do and strive to do it better."

I'm with Don Listwin, CEO of Openwave who added to the debate: "How do dominant companies lose their position? Two-thirds of the time, they pick the wrong competitor to worry about." A great point, well made.

It's important to know what your competitors are doing, but only so you differentiate yourself from them, not so that you can become a 'me too'.

Don't obsess about research

Research, like a rear-view mirror in a car, can only tell you where you've come from, not where you're going. Trying to research genuinely breakthrough category ideas is pretty near impossible since customers are notoriously bad at predicting whether they will adopt new behaviors. Sony Walkman, Bailey's Irish Cream, Post-Its, Perrier (in the UK), Red Bull and Cashpoint machines all bombed in initial research. Today, in so many areas, it is possible to get service innovation to market at light speed and turn vision into action. Steve Jobs has a supreme sense of intuition, and relies on this, not research, for creating new products like the iPad and iPhone. The real winners in the 'new normal' environment are mavericks and contrarians, prepared to follow their intuition and passion about an idea in the face of opposition, against the status quo.

A paradigm free zone

Agencies chatter enthusiastically about market paradigms more and more. The dictionary tells us it's a mindset. A formed opinion. A way of seeing the world. A particular way of thinking. A fixed pattern or model. Paradigms are, in effect, the antithesis of creativity. They discourage and eventually destroy ideas. On closer analysis, a paradigm is a set of rules that does two things: (1) it establishes or defines boundaries, and (2) in an agency context it informs the 'creative team' to behave purely within the constraints of accepted boundaries. That would be painting by numbers and that's simply not what creating a Firebrand is all about.

Be authentic

In the post credit crunch era and in a world of social networks, where all of an organization's actions and motivations are laid bare, only those companies which are genuine, transparent and live their values will achieve trust and be able to re-kindle their ambitions. Your mission, your passion, must be authentic. And you have to stay true to it. No matter what.

As Al and Laura Reis said: "The crucial ingredient in the success of any brand is its claim to authenticity".

Making a difference

These days, it's not enough to be different; you need to make a difference. Last month, I noticed a sign hanging in a CEO's office that featured the words of business strategist, Gary Hamel: "Create a cause, not a business." Businesses would do well to draw strength and courage from allegiance to a purpose. If you are pursuing your passion, so much the better.

Every Firebrand has a powerful central idea, sometimes referred to as its core essence. They have unique and differentiated value propositions that are relevant to their customers, lighting them up. Customers gain trust in their brand story because they experience it at every level of engagement.

Branding is not about 'spin'. Integrity must be at the heart of your brand. It doesn't matter what industry you are in, or what products or services you provide, if the brand story doesn't ring true or is superficial, because the company doesn't really 'own' it, then your customers and employees will see through it. If you remain true to your brand, then they will get behind it, live it and really love it.

What's Your Burning Ambition?

"When you discover your mission, you will feel its demand. It will fill you with enthusiasm and a burning desire to get to work on it."

W. Clement Stone

Ask any successful entrepreneur and they will tell you that there are a few moments in business life that they look back on as being pivotal. I've just spent the day with Mike Harris, one of the few people ever to create three multi-billion pound iconic brands: Egg plc, the UK's first online bank; First Direct, the world's first telephone banking operation and Mercury Communications, the UK's second largest telecommunications operator.

The first question Mike asked me was certainly the most challenging I've ever faced: "Win or lose, what is the big game you would love to play in the next 3 - 5 years?"

He related that, from his experience, whilst every business does not necessarily have to be an iconic brand, to be successful, it does have to *behave* like one.

Mike said that at First Direct, he and his team built the brand around the central proposition of "heroic customer service that left people feeling totally taken care of." The brand experience was the heart of his company, the driving force behind its culture.

He leant over the desk to me, looked me in the eye and told me with a quiet assurance that he believes that my consultancy's brand is all about leaving people feeling 'buzzed' from the energy of our ideas.

This, over the next few hours, translated into our perfect pitch and indeed helped to spark the inspiration for this book.

The point is that you don't need to be the size and scale of Apple or Virgin to create a vision, which shapes every action you take and gets you out of bed every morning fired up. Your vision can include the relentless search for new ideas to meet appropriate (and currently unmet) needs and wants of customers. Essentially, as Mike says, "it's about creating a brand experience and a culture that is addictive, infectious and, ultimately, irresistible."

The word 'brand' is derived from the Old Norse *brandr* meaning 'to burn.' It refers to the practice of producers burning their mark (or brand) onto their products. Now, what's your burning ambition?

Step 1 - Tinder

*"Anything that can cause a spark
in these tinder-dry conditions
will ignite it."*

Gene Madden

The Rules of Firecraft

*"Here is Edward Bear, coming downstairs
now, bump, bump, bump, on the back of
his head, behind Christopher Robin.
It is, as far as he knows, the only way of
coming downstairs, but sometimes he feels
that there really is another way, if only he
could stop bumping for a moment
and think of it."*

Perhaps surprisingly, the opening line of the much-loved children's classic, *Winnie the Pooh*, offers a very clear message to marketers. After the past few years' frenetic, jarring market activity, NOW is the time to find a place to sit and think – to take time out to plan effectively, consider alternatives objectively and then act decisively on your marketing approach.

Leslie Bland, ex-Managing Director of Close Invoice Finance, said something to me a few years ago that I have never forgotten: "Take time to work ON your business, rather than just in your business." It's something that we have taken to heart both with our agency and our approach to our clients' marketing.

Why just bump along? Doing nothing may seem an easy option right now - the reality is that it's not the most comfortable option for your business long-term.

Just like making a fire, there's a time to take stock and there are a number of conditions that have to be just right. It is essential that the top team be genuinely committed to investing time and budget to a repositioning strategy. Resources need to be allocated on their ability to deliver the strategy and the strategic intent should form the basis of all communication inside and outside the organization.

Then your most talented (remarkable) and most appropriate (relevant) people should be leading your key strategic objectives. Their individual performance, and the collective performance of the top team, should be directly based on implementing the repositioning strategy. The key performance indicators (KPIs) should reflect the strategy, as should the associated rewards and bonuses.

Brandstorming tips

Clients tell me that one of the things that they love about the Light Your Firebrand™ Workshop is that it represents a safe, non-judgmental environment where they can brainstorm new ideas, without getting burned!

Brainstorming is an idea-generating technique pioneered by the famous ad-man Alex Osborn, by which a group attempts to find a solution for a specific problem by generating the maximum number of ideas from its members.

Fire and ice

You often hear about athletes 'getting in the zone' before achieving the most incredible performance times; business people need to do that too, particularly where there is a group dynamic. 'Brandstorming', as we call it, is a fantastic icebreaker that enables you to prime the participants to get creative and start to think about the business in a fresh and inspiring way. Book a meeting room at a time everyone you would like to be involved can make and make sure that you have pens, flip chart, notepads and yellow stickies at the ready.

Appoint a facilitator (this could be you) to ensure the Brandstorming Guidelines are being met. Then assign a scribe, whose job it is to capture all of those amazing ideas.

Here are a few examples:

> If your brand were a color, what color would it be?

> If your brand were a vehicle, what make and model of vehicle would it be?

> If your brand were an actor, what actor would it be?

> If your brand were a city, what city would it be?

> If your brand were a flavor, what flavor would it be?

> If your brand were clothing, what clothing would it be?

> If your brand were a movie, what movie would it be?

> If your brand were an animal, what animal would it be?

> If your brand were a surprise present, how would your partner react?

Once you have broken the ice with these questions, you can be ready to ask the really serious ones, such as:

> What do you see as your brand values?

What do you see as your competitors' brand values?

What are the gaps / differences?

Some simple rules

- No distractions.
- Mobiles off, including Smartphone email browsing!
- Generate the maximum volume of ideas – the more the better.
- Get all of the ideas down without eliminating any of them or discussing them in any detail.
- No criticism of any idea from any member of the group, however outlandish they may seem (there's no such thing as a bad idea in a brainstorm and no evaluation is needed in this formative idea-generative phase).
- Encourage members of the group to build on the ideas of others.

Brandstorming process

The facilitator asks members to write down their ideas on yellow stickies or index cards. These are then collected, organized in clusters on a wall or desk (combining items with the same meaning) and presented to the group.

Evaluation

Straight voting (where members call out their responses in order) or dot voting (where each member is given a certain number of small sticky dots to put up next to their choices on the main list) are the most popular scoring methods.

Mind mapping tips

Mind mapping is a method of visually representing ideas and of aiding the brainstorming 'free association' process. This creative technique was developed in the 1970s by Tony Buzan, the psychologist and author. He describes mind mapping as "A method of accessing intelligence, allowing rapid expansion and exploration of an idea in note form."

Mind mapping is a very stimulating way to help people focus their innate creativity. I would go further and suggest it is therefore the most powerful way to communicate Firebrand ideas to others.

The human brain is very different from a computer. Whereas a computer works in a linear fashion, the brain works 'associatively' as well as linearly - comparing, integrating and synthesizing as it goes. The human brain is 'hard-wired' for creative thought, in that it is intrinsically a 'pattern forming' mechanism.

The creative potential of a mind map is useful in brainstorming sessions. Simply start with the basic problem or topic at the center of your sheet, and generate associations and ideas from it in order to arrive at a large number of different possible approaches. By presenting your thoughts and perceptions in a spatial manner and by using color and pictures, a better overview is gained and new connections can be made visible.

One of the reasons that mind maps are so effective is that they enable you to sketch out your main ideas very quickly (the brain loves to work at high speed!). Then, with your ideas laid out in front of you - on one page - it's easy to see the connection points and how one thought relates to another. Mind mapping is a very useful intermediate stage between the thinking process and achieving your optimum 'outcome.' This outcome could be a draft proposal; a marketing campaign; a strategic or creative rationale document; meeting notes.... as you can see, the list is endless.

When you reach for your pens and start to draw, be prepared for a few questions. I find that people are fascinated by the technique. It can become an 'icebreaker' in its own right and it is a real differentiator for your first Firebrand meeting.

If you mind map in a meeting, the interesting thing is that you will also have more time to look at the speaker - which in turn aids the listening process.

The main steps within the process are as follows:

Step 1: Our mind focuses on the center ... so mind mapping begins with a word or image that symbolizes what you want to think about placed in the middle of the page.

Step 2: Lighten Up! Mind mapping is a brain dumping process that helps stimulate new ideas and connections. Start with an open attitude to it ... you can always get serious later when you've had greater practice.

Step 3: Free Associate. Each branch or line has either one word or an image on it (or both)! As ideas emerge, print one or two word descriptions of the ideas on lines branching from the central focus. Allow the ideas to expand outward into branches and sub-branches. Put down all ideas without judgment or evaluation.

Step 4: Think Fast. Your brain works best in 5-7 minute bursts so capture that explosion of ideas as rapidly as possible. Key words, symbols and images provide a mental short-hand to help you record ideas as quickly as possible.

Step 5: Break Boundaries. Break through the 'A4 sheet mentality' that says you have to write on white, letter-size paper with black ink or pencil. Use ledger paper or easel paper or cover an entire wall with yellow stickies ... the bigger the paper, the more ideas you'll have. In the initial formatting of ideas use bright colors, fat colored markers, crayons, or skinny felt tipped pens – whatever works for you.

Step 6: Judge Not. Put everything down that comes to mind even if it is completely unrelated. If you're brainstorming ideas for a report and you suddenly remember you need to pick-up your cleaning, put down 'cleaning.' Otherwise your mind will get stuck like a record in that 'cleaning' groove and you'll never generate those great ideas.

Step 7: Keep Moving. Keep your hand moving. If ideas slow down, draw empty lines, and watch your brain automatically find ideas to put on them. Or change colors to re-energize your mind. Stand up and mind map on an easel pad to generate even more energy.

Step 8: Allow Organization. Sometimes you see relationships and connections immediately and you can add sub-branches to a main idea. Sometimes you don't, so you just connect the ideas to the central focus. Organization can always come later; the first requirement is to get the ideas out of your head and onto the paper.

Avoiding Brand Glare

"There are two kinds of light - the glow that illuminates, and the glare that obscures."

James Thurber

Branding 101

"You asked me once, what was in Room 101. I told you that you knew the answer already. Everyone knows it. The thing that is in Room 101 is the worst thing in the world."

Room 101 is a place introduced in the novel *Nineteen Eighty-Four* by George Orwell. It is a torture chamber in the Ministry of Love in which the Party attempts to subject a prisoner to his or her own worst nightmare, fear or phobia.

Here are just a few of mine:

Commitment Phobia

Is your organization reducing its commitment to marketing? Millward Brown research shows that cutting your marketing budget in a downturn will result in a weaker and much less profitable brand.

Anti-Social Media Disorder

Does your organization understand how to leverage social media or even how valuable this could be to your business? An agency that knows how to engage communities, attract user generated content and increase your online presence with knowledge of effective online strategies will open your eyes to a new world of opportunity.

Delusions of Brandeur

Do you just love your logo? Do you believe you have a beautiful web site? That's fantastic but are you placing too great a significance on your brand's look and feel over and above strategic substance? The Light Your Firebrand™ process will set you on the path to creating a brand that genuinely means something and really matters to your stakeholders. Coco Chanel summed it up perfectly – Ask yourself the question from your customer's point of view: "Why should I care about you?"

Metricism

What criteria will contribute the most to your success? What sectors and clusters of individual prospects, introducers and clients will deliver your profits next year? The scope for measurable search engine marketing and track-able, data-driven e-mail marketing campaigns is significant, blending art and science as never before. Measurement against key objectives must be applied to every aspect of your marketing - online and offline - from clicks to enquiry, through to conversion.

Clinical Sameness Syndrome

Is there anyone else in your industry that could credibly make your Brand Promise? (Tip: If you said anything about "friendly, personal service," or being "the most innovative provider of business solutions," the answer is most definitely "yes").

Getting Historical

Assumptions made when the brand was created may no longer hold true. Analyze changes in the perceptions of target markets when exploring opportunities for brand expansion, repositioning and revitalization.

Obstacles to creativity

With so much negative comment in the media, it is worthwhile being alive to some of the 'creativity blockers' that may inhibit you from being able to Light Your Firebrand™. Here are just a few:

- Inflexible strategies / unchallenged rules
- Existing paradigms / sacred cows
- Habit / routines / comfort levels
- Fear of consequences / making mistakes / change
- Not invented here syndrome
- Upbringing and beliefs at odds with your target audience
- Outdated thinking / knowledge
- Self-doubt and self-criticism
- Stress
- Boredom
- Ego
- Rational (only) thought
- Being too close to the market you serve
- Politeness

- Fear of appearing stupid / childish
- Unwillingness to play games
- Lack of time

Address these issues head-on and you are creating the business oxygen you need to Light your Firebrand™.

Preparing the Ground

"Would you tell me, please, which way
I ought to go from here".
"That depends a good deal on where you
want to get to," said the Cat.
"I don't much care where," said Alice,
"so long as I get somewhere."
"Then it doesn't matter which way you go,"
said the Cat.

Lewis Carroll, Alice in Wonderland

Too many companies are in the same predicament as Alice, unsure of what their brand stands for, and therefore uncertain of which direction to take their business. The journey starts by truly knowing your customer.

I have seen some agencies conduct brand workshops where they have been quick to talk about 'marketing destinations' and 'brand footprint' but with very little concept of who the customer actually is. It's almost as if they have taken the phrase 'supply and demand' and just applied it literally in that order. A true Firebrand generates 'demand and supply.'

A is for Audience, B is for Brand

Speaking of the order of things, Audience always comes before Brand. The other day, I was speaking to Mindy

Gibbins-Klein, 'The Book Midwife,' who has helped me enormously to organize and explore ideas for the creation of this book. Mindy told me that when writing a book, one of the very first stages is to clearly define your reader to the extent that you feel that they are in the same room as you. She encouraged me to think about precisely who my target audience is – even to the extent that I had a framed photograph of that individual on my desk. Which reminds me, it's still there!

Well, who are you?

(Who are you? Who, who, who, who?)

I really wanna know

(Who are you? Who, who, who, who?)

Tell me, who are you?

(Who are you? Who, who, who, who?)

'Cause I really wanna know

(Who are you? Who, who, who, who?)

The Who

Famous lyrics and an inspired choice for the memorable opening sequence for the show CSI. More importantly, the credo of every Firebrand strategist. You have to know exactly who you are talking to, otherwise how do you know what to say. Beyond just their demographics (age, gender, geography) you really need to know who they are on the inside.

Exercise 1 - Knowing Your Customer

Our goal is twofold:

1. To create the broadest description of your target audience possible

2. To keep it narrow enough to be relevant.

Use the following headings to paint an insightful picture of the people you wish to communicate with:

Age

Gender

Geography

Job title / position

Leisure interests – books, hobbies, sports

Tribes – clubs, groups

Strategic alliances, partners and joint ventures

What are their corporate goals?

What are their personal goals?

Organization and organizational style

Attitudes and behaviors

Values and beliefs

Hopes and aspirations

Problems and concerns

Once you've established precisely to whom you will be talking and the interests that they have in common, you can start to define what's important to them.

The TOWS matrix

With a firm view of your customer in mind, the next step is to quickly identify where you are now and determine where your journey will take you next. You may have used a SWOT analysis before. If you haven't, it is a really simple and effective way of looking as objectively as possible at your strengths, weaknesses, opportunities and threats.

A SWOT analysis identifies:

- What the business does well
- How it could improve
- Whether it is taking full advantage of the opportunities (particularly those that match with strengths)
- Whether there are any changes in the environment which require a corresponding change in business strategy

It is important to remember that strengths and weaknesses are internal factors, whereas opportunities and threats are external. When I am facilitating a Light Your Firebrand™ workshop, I always ask the management team to split into manageable groups (I find a maximum of six people is ideal) just to quickly set down the external factors first so we can get to grips with the environment we're operating in, using the internal factors to help address them later. This management tool is known as the TOWS Matrix.

Exercise 2 – Dipping Your TOWS

List your threats, opportunities, weaknesses and strengths in the matrix below:

TOWS Analysis

THREATS	OPPORTUNITIES

WEAKNESSES	STRENGTHS

Here's an example of a completely fictitious TOWS Analysis on an organization:

Threats

- Loss of key personnel (incentivize, attractive contracts, bonuses for high performers)

- Greater transparency driving down margins (unique value proposition to justify 'reassuringly expensive' tag, bundling products making it more difficult to compare or strip out services that customers don't care about)

- Increasing marketing activity from competitors with larger budgets (stay even closer - relationship building, enhanced services, regular contact)

- Competitors buying business through reciprocity and high commissions (faster turnaround, greater certainty)

- Challenging economy could drift into market stagnancy (focus on areas of critical need)

- Regulation a possibility (be part of the debate, lobbying)

- High prices for potential acquisitions (may fall in more challenging times - monitor).

- Departure of the manufacturing industry as a key source of business (focus on new, alternative sectors where there are signs of growth)

Opportunities

- Fragmented markets offer opportunities for organic growth and expansion through acquisitions.

- Acquisition of key competitors for economies of scale and to increase distribution and product spread

- Competitors are bureaucratic and slow

- Legal changes about loan structures in our favor

- Focus on markets where speed is valued, such as turnarounds, restructures and management buy outs
- Restricted liquidity elsewhere in the market opens up significant opportunities
- Use of automated systems to create a short-term competitive advantage
- Product development with alliances for specific industry types
- Good personnel at competitors have been made redundant
- New systems will allow greater volume of deals to be handled

Weaknesses

- No succession planning (identify and nurture talent)
- Little strategic planning (start brand planning now using this book)
- No natural lead flow from parent company (explore alternatives)
- No branch network (partner)
- No European network (partner / joint venture)
- Not enough sales people in key geographical territories (recruit / partner)
- No ability to provide reciprocal business for introducers (create the opportunity to do so / find value elsewhere)

- New projects have distracted management team from core service areas (improve planning / delegate)
- More expensive than competitors (build / strengthen / communicate value proposition)

Strengths

- Unique value proposition (relevant differentiation)
- Robust business model
- Strong parent company
- Speed to market with new ideas
- Ability to make faster decisions
- Access to highly experienced, qualified people
- Track record of delivering our promises
- Broad customer base and presence in profitable markets, restricting exposure levels
- Established business relationships
- Product innovation
- Centralized underwriting – consistency of decision making
- Founder member of trade body
- Latest automated systems, leading to greater efficiency and reduced customer administration

Exercise 3 - Grinding Out the Strategic Base

Once you have established your TOWS lists, split into different groups to identify the following strategies and then bring these back to the boardroom:

SO strategies - Use your firm's internal strengths to take advantage of external opportunities (capitalize / crush strategies).

WO strategies - Improve internal weaknesses by taking advantage of external opportunities (improve / change strategies).

ST strategies - Utilize your strengths to avoid, reduce or eliminate the impact of external threats (monitor / anticipate strategies).

WT strategies - Adopt defensive tactics directed at reducing internal weaknesses and, where possible, avoiding external threats (eliminate / reduce strategies).

You may find it helpful to plot your thoughts using the following matrix:

STRATEGIES

SO	WO
CAPITALIZE / CRUSH	IMPROVE / CHANGE

ST	WT
MONITOR / ANTICIPATE	ELIMINATE / REDUCE

Now you have a better idea of your business in the context of its environment, it is time to look at your competitors.

Why should somebody choose you over your competition other than price? The answer to this question may help you choose the best position upon which to build a strong brand.

There may be many possible positions for your brand but it is important to choose the one that is most defendable, least likely to be copied, most compelling, and most unique. Do not try to incorporate so many points of differentiation in your positioning that your customers become confused or overwhelmed. This might cause competition with yourself, cannibalize sales of your higher profit offering(s), and be very difficult to manage.

What makes your company preferred in the minds of your clients and prospects might be something in the product, something in your people, or maybe even some strongly held corporate belief or philosophy.

Exercise 4 – Closer to the Competition

To distance your business from your competitors, you first need to get a whole lot closer to them. You can make a positive start by visiting the web sites of your top 5 competitors.

Read their intro copy on their home page

Read your intro copy on your home page

Ask yourself if any of the companies (yours included) really stand out from the others

Which ones are targeting the same market as you?

What are their selling points?

What are their strengths and weaknesses?

Can you identify any market trends you need to take account of?

The 8 Ps

McCarthy famously identified Four Ps in the range of options open to manipulation by marketers. These were product, price, promotion and place. Today, marketers augment the mix with the additional three Ps (people, process and physical evidence) and increasingly add partners.

Exercise 5 – In The Mixer

Now set out the service marketing mix - the 8Ps - for your business and your top 5 competitors. These include:

1. Product (or service name and description).

2. Price (pricing, discounts, payment terms).

3. Promotion (various ways of communicating to the customer).

4. Place (online and offline presence - websites and locations).

5. People (Board, staff – number, roles and quality).

6. Process (sales process, order process, flow of activities).

7. Physical evidence (the experience of using a product or service, plus the videos and litera-ture that enhance that experience).

8. Partners (indirect channels - alliances, part-nerships, affinity schemes, joint ventures).

Set this information out on a simple matrix and you will be able to identify at a glance what it is about your company that's different from your competi-tors and build on those strengths.

Write down the points of parity – those category benefits that are critical for establishing credibility but are the base level of performance expectations. Then note the points of difference – those ideas from your brand and competing brands that are the most meaningful and potentially distinctive.

Tinder Chapter Challenge

In the process of searching for Tinder, we have:

1. Gained a clear understanding of why repositioning and brand revitalization are imperatives
   for our business.

2. Established a deeper understanding and
   appreciation of our customers and their needs.

3. Identified the threats and opportunities facing
   our business.

4. Focused on developing specific strategies
   to meet these challenges, maximizing our
   strengths and minimizing / eliminating our
   weaknesses.

5. Mapped out how we differ from our top five
   competitors at each point of the marketing mix.

Step 2 - Spark

"Without inspiration the best powers of the mind remain dormant, there is a fuel in us which needs to be ignited with sparks."

Johann Gottfried Von Herder

Illuminating Your Difference

*"The questions which one asks oneself
begin, at least, to illuminate the world,
and become one's key to the experience of
others."*

James Arthur Baldwin

As Seth Godin observed in his book, *Purple Cow: Transform Your Business by Being Remarkable,* the key to success is to find a way to stand out - to be the 'purple cow' in a field of monochrome Holsteins. The key word here is not 'different' but 'remarkable' – that people will actually 'remark upon' that point of difference and therefore spread the word. When I read that a marketing agency had called itself 'Purple Cow,' I couldn't help feeling that somehow they had really missed the point here!

In a recent study, 81% of professional service firms reported they used differentiation as a marketing approach in the previous three years; the majority thought of it as an exercise in image enhancement. However, the most-used surface-level differentiation approaches were not necessarily found to be the most effective. The more operationally 'deep' the differentiation strategies were, the more successful they proved to be and the less price became an issue in the decision-making process. It's great to stand out but there needs to be a connected marketing reason to support and substantiate the differentiated proposition.

The first P

We've taken a look together at the 8Ps of the marketing mix. However, I believe that the modern, integrated marketing mix must have a powerful 'first P,' one that is just as credible and which really matters to people: positioning.

Without effective positioning, organizations become commodity driven, unable to command sustainable growth and superior profitability.

Positioning is the strategic ownership of exclusive value in the hearts and minds of your customers, enabling your brand to occupy a distinct position, relative to competing brands. It's what gives them reasons to buy your brand, to be loyal to your business, to be an active referral source for you. Tangible products & services benefits form the proof points that support your positioning and make it believable - but a truly strong positioning goes beyond these tangible factors, making powerful and emotive connections.

Finding these emotional connections is what turns a product or service into a Firebrand.

Which reminds me of this short story:

One day, there was a blind man sitting on the steps of a building with a hat by his feet and a sign that read: 'I am blind, please help.' A branding expert was walking by and stopped to observe. He saw that the blind man had only a few coins in his hat. He dropped in more coins and, without asking for permission, took the sign and rewrote it.

He returned the sign to the blind man and left. That afternoon the branding expert returned to the blind man and noticed that his hat was full of notes and coins.

The blind man recognized his footsteps and asked if it was he who had rewritten his sign and wanted to know what he had written on it.

The branding specialist responded: "Nothing that was not true. I just wrote the message a little differently." He smiled and went on his way.

The new sign read: 'Today is Spring and I cannot see it.'

By positioning your brand competitively in the market - and evocatively inside the hearts and minds of target clients - you are giving them reasons:

to buy your brand;

to be loyal to your business;

to become an active referral source for you.

A Firebrand achieves this by:

Taking ownership of a truly remarkable, unique point of difference, benefit or attribute.

Establishing a reputation for consistent delivery of that differential proposition.

Reinventing your business to deliver your unique value proposition in a highly relevant way that meets the needs of your clients and the process by which you interact with them.

Creating a heightened emotional connection with your clients at every level of engagement.

From Positioning to Oppositioning

"For every action, there is an equal and opposite reaction."

Sir Isaac Newton

Do you recall seeing Lewis Hamilton lead from pole position to chequered flag in Indianapolis? The key moments that defined his victory were played out in a split second.

A car spins ahead of the pack. The other drivers hesitate or brake to avoid collision. Hamilton instantly, instinctively accelerates, not just as an avoidance strategy, but to maintain a commanding lead.

What does this analogy mean for your business? After all, we've been operating in an environment where 'business at the speed of thought,' as Bill Gates has defined it, is considered the norm. Current strategies may prove enough to survive but to truly thrive in a hardening economy requires a more robust and, it could be said, more radical positioning – '**Oppositioning**.'

Similarly, Carlos Sastre of Spain claimed that he rode like two men to clinch his first win in the Tour de France from eight starts. His achievement makes for a strong marketing analogy for these challenging times.

The climb up Alpe d'Huez is 13.8 km at an average gradient of 7.9% with 21 hairpin bends (les 21 virages) - the toughest stage of the grueling 3,500km race. Sastre deliberately selected that time and stage to make his move ahead of the main group of riders – the 'Peloton.'

"I suffered a lot on the way to the summit, but I take great pleasure in capturing the jersey," Sastre said through a translator. "A pure climber has to take advantage of his opportunities, and this was mine."

His decision as to when and where he would move ahead defined him as a true champion. This is not the time to keep your head down and just do enough to make it in a tough climate. Now is the time to focus on how you are going to thrive, not just survive. It's time to get as far ahead of your own 'Peloton' as you can be when the economy rallies.

Terrill and Middlebrooks, authors of *Market Leadership Strategies*, agree with these disruptive, oppositional principles:

"To build a strong brand, service companies must implement their brand with hard-hitting positioning strategies that differ significantly from competitors. In fact, most powerful differentiation strategies are directly opposite from those of primary competitors."

In *Blue Ocean Strategy: How to Create Uncontested Market Space and Make the Competition Irrelevant* (Harvard Business School Press), W. Chan Kim and Renée Mauborgne challenge everything you thought you knew about the requirements for strategic success, and instead argue that the way to win is to stop competing. The key is to be acutely aware of but not obsessive about your immediate competition.

One way of looking at this is to adopt a 'blue ocean' strategy.

Many companies settle for a remorseless battle for success in a commoditized 'red ocean' or shrinking profit pool. In the red ocean, industry boundaries are defined and accepted, prices are driven lower, and the competitive rules of the game become more apparent. As the market space becomes increasingly crowded, Kim and Mauborgne argue that companies need to use an 'opposite approach.' Instead of benchmarking the competition, brand pioneers set their own rules and create 'blue oceans' of uncontested market space.

'Oppositioning' is one of the most successful competitive strategies ever to be unleashed on a cluttered marketplace. Yet, it is just one step on your journey towards having a Firebrand.

Exercise 6 - Contrary Creative Techniques

When you are looking at your opportunities and threats, try some of these contrary, creative techniques. It is incredible what truths they can unveil.

Look for extreme gaps. Figure out what everybody else is not doing. Then see how you may be able to turn that gap into a distinctive competitive advantage.

State your problem or opportunity in reverse. It's far easier to think negatively. List all the ways you could make customer services bad, how you would set about decreasing sales or even establish what would make a poor product.

Then reverse your thought process again. What would you learn from this exercise that you could apply to your business?

Try to define what something is not. Search thesaurus antonyms. By looking at the attributes that are inconsistent or oppositional to your brand, product or service, you can define what your brand represents in the minds of your clients with far greater clarity.

Chinese philosopher, Lao-tzu wrote: "The wise leader knows how to be creative. In order to lead, the leader learns to follow. In order to prosper, the leader learns to live simply. In both cases, it is the interaction that is creative."

Back to front thinking

I've had some fascinating meetings in the past two weeks focused on attracting sellers to online marketplaces and B2B portal sites. It is perfectly logical that every marketing dollar has been spent focusing on communicating and promoting services to sellers to attract them to these communities, since that is what drives the revenue models.

In times where there is some disequilibrium in the buyer / seller equation through purchaser scarcity, the real driver to growth may be found in disruptive thinking. What if budgetary spend on attracting sellers were to be reversed? What if we concentrated on getting the largest community of buyers for that marketplace. Create that community, that interest group, that tribe and it could be argued that vendors will queue round the block for that kind of access to a premium buyer marketplace.

What else could you achieve by back to front marketing thinking?

Every attribute, concept or idea gains a heightened contextual meaning through the relationship it has with its opposite. Now is a good time for organizations to learn to see things backwards, inside out, and upside down - a strategic position that to me suggests the antithesis of failure.

Exercise 7 - The 5S Scenarios

We are often asked about the techniques we use as a branding consultancy for brainstorming differential strategic models. Here are five of the most powerful approaches we use to develop 'What If' scenarios:

Substitute

What happens if I substitute product, price, promotion or place?

Synergy

What materials, features, processes, people, products or components can I combine?

Selection

Which parts or characteristics of the product/ process could I change, add, simplify or delete?

Stretch

Can I put my current solution/ product/ process to other purposes, potentially in other markets?

Swap

How can I change, reorder or reverse my processes, product delivery or marketing sequence?

Pearls of wisdom?

I went out for a drink with a friend this evening, after what had been a long but inspiring week. Our discussions got around to his business and the opportunities for expansion and the specific issues of capacity that he was facing. I quizzed him for a while and he told me that he appreciated the fact that I don't shy away from asking the tough questions - the uncomfortable, challenging ones. I'm beginning to think that is the spark-point for most successful creative ideas.

Grit may be uncomfortable and irritating. It's also the source of a pearl. No grit, no jewel. Only the perfect alignment of strategy and creativity can ever result in a gem of an idea.

However, it must be remembered that not many oysters grow a pearl. It all depends on capturing the right bit of grit - asking the right question, demanding the right responses. Apart from its role in growing a pearl, grit also hints at a focused mind, an invincible spirit and an unyielding courage and fortitude.

Drilling for oil

What made Jean Paul Getty wealthy was his tenacity and commitment to drill further and deeper than anyone else had ever done before him. Not content with discovering an oil seam, Getty just didn't stop drilling around the area until he found a bigger seam and then another and another. Most entrepreneurs and their investors would have been more than content with 1 million barrels a year from a plot of land, Getty wasn't and kept on until the equivalent plot yielded an astonishing 16 million barrels a year.

Are you like Jean Paul Getty? Do you maximize every business opportunity? Do you ask all of the questions you could do? Would asking three times the number of questions yield three times the opportunity?

Many companies I know are content with 'striking oil,' getting the initial new business win. They work hard, satisfy the client's business requirement and move on. The issue is that had they asked more questions at the outset they would have discovered several other projects, perhaps even more lucrative than the first.

You can get away with a new business strategy in good times, even prosper with the right momentum. In these times when the pipeline may be slower, when firms merge, sectors polarize and the number of players in the market is reduced, there is even more reason to cross-sell and up-sell than ever before.

JP Getty said: "To succeed in business, to reach the top, an individual must know all it is possible to know about that business." The same can be said for your clients' needs.

Exercise 8 – A Question of Leadership

Consider those attributes in the list below where you can command a leadership position. Which are transient and which are the most sustainable?

Which of these when bundled together offer your business an unassailable competitive advantage?

Pioneer - first to market

Modernity - latest to market

Innovation / creativity

Design / style / image/ packaging

Ease of ordering

Market share / size (within segment)

Technology / pathfinder

Manufacture / process

Quality / reliability

Service / responsiveness

Flexibility

Speed of delivery

Relationship / channel partners

Prestige / exclusivity

Sector knowledge / specialization

Technical expertise

Product enhancement / bundling

Global / international

Regional / local

Bargain / cheapest

Payment terms

Guarantees / reduce risk

Value / superior cost benefit

Please note that I have not used 'longevity' as a leadership criteria, yet how often do we read words like 'established in 1854,' as the opening sentence in corporate literature!

Northern Rock Building Society was formed in 1965. Lehman Brothers was established in 1850. Bradford Equitable Building Society and the Bingley Building Society, both established in 1851, merged in 1964. Washington Mutual was founded on September 25, 1889. To see the downfall of any institution with a lengthy history is tragic but, as we have seen, market conditions do not respect the age of any of these organizations.

Clients no longer care that XYZ Bank was established in 1871 or ABC Accountants was founded in 1980. It says nothing about the quality of the organization or its competitive advantage and it takes up valuable mind space. Space that should be reserved for the core essence of your brand and your unique value propositions in the context of how these help your client.

Why then are organizations (particularly accountancy firms) so keen to put the number of years they have been trading as the first thing we see on their web sites? This is weak, bland and uninteresting and is wholly irrelevant to their marketing effort.

Take a leaf out of Grant Thornton's book: "A brand is one of the most powerful tools that an organization can use to communicate accountability and leadership wherever it does business. We have created this new brand to support our global business strategy of demonstrating real leadership within our profession and becoming a more cohesive global organization." David McDonnell, Grant Thornton

The One and Only

"You do not merely want to be considered just the best of the best. You want to be considered the only ones who do what you do."

Jerry Garcia, lead singer of the Grateful Dead

You have prepared the ground, gathering your tinder and putting it into a neat pile, and I would imagine you'll have an abundance of different ideas sparking around already.

However, before you go any further, consider this: Why would they choose 'A' company when they could work with 'THE' company that meets their specific needs?

Are you merely:

A business amongst many?

Or are you:

<u>THE</u> 'go to' business in your chosen niche.

What would it take? Would your promise fulfill our proven criteria of being relevant, remarkable, reputational and real?

From A to "THE"

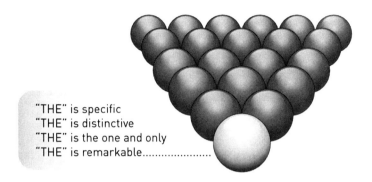

"THE" is specific
"THE" is distinctive
"THE" is the one and only
"THE" is remarkable......................

Think about it from your clients' point of view. Why would you choose just 'A' supplier?

'A' is generic. 'A' is me-too. 'A' is one of many. 'A' is just ok.

'THE' is specific. 'THE' is distinctive. 'THE' is the one and only. 'THE' is remarkable.

'THE' commands share of mind and wallet – 'THE' accountant who deals with all of our finances. 'THE' bank that fulfils all our lending needs. 'THE' leasing company that funds our fleet.

Or taking one of my clients as an example: 'Pharmacy Partners is THE only dedicated pharmacy finance specialist in the UK.'

Think carefully about your niche. Is it an inch wide and a mile deep? If so, it may be incredibly profitable to mine your niche leadership position further.

Exercise 9 – From A to The

Try to complete the following statement truthfully. Take your time. Don't get discouraged. This is difficult and may require a number of iterations before you feel comfortable with it. Revisit it as many times as you feel you need to – no one said it would be easy.

For (your target audience), our company (brand) is the only (what you do / descriptor of business) that delivers / offers / guarantees / creates / understands (statement of key benefit or guiding value), because we believe (key reason to believe), which makes our customers feel (emotional response).

Kipling's Lesson

To start to develop your positioning statement, I have enlisted the help of Kipling's *Six Honest Serving-Men*, though not quite in the order that they appear in the poem:

> *"I keep six honest serving-men*
> *(They taught me all I knew);*
> *Their names are What and Why and When*
> *And How and Where and Who."*

Exercise 10 – Six Honest Serving-Men

Why (I believe...)

What (I have a passion for / I want to be famous for...)

Who (I love working with...)

How (The process we have created is...)

Where (I work regionally / nationally / globally, online / offline...)

When (My product / service is ideally suited to the time when...)

When you have completed this book, it would be energizing to revisit this exercise to see how far you and your Firebrand have come. I'm confident that you'll be amazed at the clarity, purpose and passion of your brand proposition.

The Source of the Flame

"For light I go directly to the Source of light,
not to any of the reflections."
Peace Pilgrim

You know your business. You know your audience. However, articulating how they feel about your brand in an authentic, meaningful and innovative way is always challenging.

Entrepreneur and ex-Dragon's Den investor, Doug Richards said at a trade association conference in Venice: "If you can't decimate an industry, what good is an innovation." I believe that the challenge of innovation is an individual as well as a collective one – that focus on a distinctive attribute or 'core essence' is brand-shaping and potentially market-shifting. Innovation, not imitation is the way forward to sustainable brand value.

Your Core Essence is the DNA that runs through your business and makes you distinct from your competitors (how you do things, what you want your customer to feel, not just what you do).

A Firebrand is about intense focus. If you were to bottle what you have that is unique and then distil it into just one word, what would that look like?

Riding a Harley-Davidson motorcycle feels 'liberating.' Exploring Walt Disney World with your children feels 'magical.' What word do you wish to own in your individual customer's mind?

> *"People don't ask for facts in making up their minds. They would rather have one, good soul-satisfying emotion than a dozen facts."*
>
> **Robert Keith Leavitt**

Exercise 11 – Soul Searching

List your product and service offerings

List customer needs (emotional and tangible) that are met through these.

List terms that describe how you think your company is currently perceived by your clients and your industry – positive and negative. Take your time and try to come up with as many as you can. Ask colleagues, clients and suppliers that you are close to and add their comments to the list.

Make a second list, this time using words that describe how you'd like your company to be perceived by your clients and your industry. Be honest and aspirational. Reach high. You may come up with some inspiring descriptions that don't match up with your business right now, but that you'd really like to work towards. Go ahead and put them down too.

Take the most positive words and select the top five that are most important to you. Having said that, they don't need to be clever words at this stage. I mean, don't put us out of a job! They just need to be the words that you most want to own in your customers' hearts and minds.

Try to avoid generic terms, such as 'professional' and 'best' and stay well away from descriptive words that name the product or service. Now test these words against the following criteria:

Exercise 12 – The Meaningful Matrix

Relevant

It may be aspirational but it ultimately must pass the test of truth and be capable of being delivered. Can your organization truly deliver on the word you have selected?

Remarkable

A Firebrand is unique, so has to celebrate a different attribute from your competitors. Is your brand the one and only brand in your market that has this word at its heart?

Reputational

The essence must be credible or the brand will be rejected. To find out what your customers believe about your brand, ask them. It's okay for the brand essence to be aspirational, but do your customers believe you can deliver on the proposition?

Real

A Firebrand distils and conveys a strong emotional connection. What does your brand leave your customers feeling at every touch point? Can your organization deliver value to the same high standards and sustain it - person to person, day in day out?

Connecting to your core

A brand is vacuous as a customer promise, unless and until it becomes a core business purpose. Your Core Brand Essence is the brand's promise, distilled and expressed in the simplest, most single-minded terms - a single word or phrase that captures the soul of your brand.

This is to be your guiding ethos, driving your value proposition, shaping your business culture and providing the platform to connect more powerfully with your customers and employees at a deeper level of emotional engagement.

Everything that is done in your brand's name should be both a confirmation and celebration of your Core Brand Essence. For those who serve the brand, it is a beacon that motivates and inspires continued commitment.

Exercise 13 – Connecting to Your Core

Make a start by drawing four concentric circles on a piece of paper and put a single attribute (one word or two word phrase) at the center.

This word or short phrase must stand up to detailed examination, satisfying the following criteria:

- Meaningful
- Clear
- Compelling
- Communicable
- Own-able
- Relevant
- Sustainable
- Energizing

Inner Core

Your Core Brand Essence defines the qualities, characteristics, personality and uniqueness of your brand. It embodies its core competencies, advantages, culture and values. It characterizes what your brand stands for in the minds of your customers and stakeholders. Ultimately, it articulates what you want your brand to be famous for!

Using the Soul Searching and Meaningful Matrix Exercises as your foundation, list five key advantages of your product or service and put these in the Inner Core. What are the most vital aspects of your service promise from your customers' point of view? What would your customers really miss if your brand did not exist? What do you do that is different from your competitors? What do you do better than the rest? Do the words you have listed in the Inner Core support or link to your Core Brand Essence? What do your top five attributes look like in that context?

Outer Core

The Outer Core consists of the remaining attributes you have brainstormed that are important aspects of your service offering, but which do not feature at the true heart of your brand as you have defined it. If these were no longer there, your brand would still have its compelling purpose.

No-Go Areas

Your No-Go Areas form an exclusion zone. As you will see later, it is vital to define what you do not stand for as well as what you do. The best place to start is the flip-side of your Core Brand Essence and Inner Core combined. If you have determined that your Core Brand Essence is 'Agility', then 'Slow', 'Unresponsive' and 'Inflexible' might appear in your list of No-Go Areas.

Core Essence

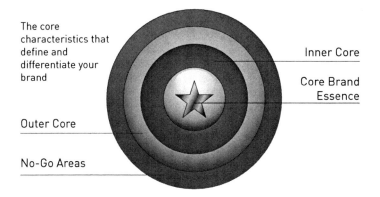

The core characteristics that define and differentiate your brand

Inner Core

Core Brand Essence

Outer Core

No-Go Areas

To show you that we practice what we preach, we will now take a look at the core brand essence for Strand Financial. At the center of our offering are the words 'Inspired and Informed', which is exactly how we want to leave our clients feeling.

This forms our Core Brand Essence and additional aspects of our brand characteristics are featured around it. Examples of no-go areas for this brand would be 'dull', 'me-too', 'tired', 'unclear' and 'uncommunicative'.

Core Essence

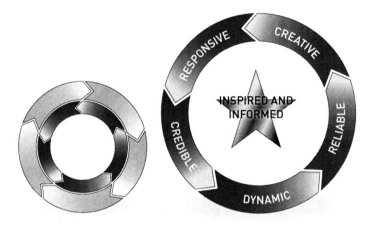

Where Core Essence becomes the strapline

Your brand doesn't need to have a strapline or tagline but we have developed a number of brands where the core essence has led to this naturally: From 'drawing on experience' and 'lending energy' to 'lending responsively' (asset based lenders) and from 'deeply relevant' (semantic search) to 'effortless transparency' (automated data transfer), each brand will have its own distinctive and crystal clear focus.

Know your brand boundaries

First coined by architect Ludwig Mies van der Rohe, the phrase, "less is more," is perfectly attuned to the brand building needs of today. "As provocative as it sounds," said CEO Helmut Panke of BMW, "the biggest task in brand-building is being able to say 'No!'"

Say 'No!' by pruning products, multiple messages and marginal media.

To illustrate this point in my keynote speech at the Annual Business Money Conference, I told a story about tourists walking through a small Indian village. As they approached a clearing, they noticed a little old man by the side of the road. He was reaching down and picking up scraps of wood. When they gathered closer to the man, they observed that he was producing the most beautiful elephant figurines. They watched fascinated as he whittled away at the wood with such skill, speed and dexterity. A lady broke away from the crowd and asked the question that was on everyone's lips: "Excuse me. I couldn't help wondering how you are able to create such wonderful figurines at such speed using just a rusty penknife?" The old man looked her straight in the eye and said, "It's really quite simple. I just cut away all the bits that don't look like an elephant."

If you want to protect your business and emerge stronger, the answer is simple - you need to cut out all the parts that don't look like your brand – then focus and build on what remains. Focus on what's core. Eliminate ruthlessly.

Mind engine optimisation

I'm a fervent believer in search engine optimization (SEO). I've seen what it can do for our financial clients who are enjoying page one rankings in Google for key industry search terms and consequently driving record levels of quality enquiry. However, I'm also an advocate of MEO – **mind engine optimization**. Here, clients approach their browsers with your brand already in pole position in their mental search engine.

In the marketing classic, *Positioning* by Al Ries and Jack Trout it says, in essence:

- Position yourself in the prospect's mind
- Convey just one single message
- Set yourself apart from your competitors
- Sacrifice by virtue of being focused on one thing

I agree with the first point entirely; a Firebrand is first created in the mind before it can ever be created in the market. On the second point, I also concur that you will gain by standing for one attribute that will give you competitive advantage. However, and this is a big however, there is also a valid point that could be argued that in this era of hyper-competition, 'bundling' can also form a powerful unique value proposition, where multiple attributes culminate in a hybrid proposition. Regarding the third point, by this stage I'm sure you're well aware of the importance I attach to differentiation! So, the first three get my vote, with perhaps some adjustment.

I have to say that the fourth assumption leaves me cold and from my experience I believe it to be fundamentally wrong on every level. The principle of sacrifice, of potentially missing out, has left countless marketers reluctant to use a distinctive single-minded proposition that, if applied, would doubtless prove highly successful. Here's my point and one of the main secrets of branding success:

Just because you are known for and exclusively focused on one attribute doesn't have to mean that you have to give up all others.

Less is more

Consider the following real-life example from the world of financial marketing:

A large regional accountancy firm that has earned an unrivalled reputation for delivering complex mergers and acquisitions work has won more standard audit work from clients than its competitors. The key is held in the thought-process of the prospects themselves. It follows that if the firm can handle work that is that complex and exacting, the attributes of expertise, added value, professionalism, timeliness, accuracy etc will be applied to the entire brand experience and specifically the approach to the audit. It's a view that flies in the face of commonly accepted marketing theory, that by becoming even more focused, you actually gain greater diversity of opportunity in your market! I can definitely say from my own experience, that Strand Financial's niche focus has brought the business into the inner circle of our industry – so we see more interesting branding projects.

Mark Twain summed it up perfectly: "I cannot give you a formula for success, but I can give you a formula for failure, which is: try to please everybody."

Lead the line

Recently, I was talking to an MBA friend of mine, debating market leadership strategy. He posed the question whether differentiation was a function of leadership or whether leadership was a function of differentiation. At university it was taught that differentiation was a strategy of leadership. Yet, we concluded that without clear and continued differentiation, you couldn't lead a market in a sustainable manner.

We went further to say that differentiation is not just the focus or purpose of marketing, it is marketing! Without the ability to make a real difference, there can be no leadership, no competitive advantage, and no ability to shift a market.

Being number one

Making a difference in the marketplace is THE imperative marketing strategy for today. As Peter Thompson, business and personal growth strategist would say, "Your take on it" is the make-or-break virtue in this era of hyper-competition.

What does it mean to be number one in your market? That depends on what your market is. To have meaning, differentiation has to matter to your market or market segments. For example, you may not be able to claim market leadership within the leasing market. However, you may be the legitimate market leader in vendor leasing for forklift trucks and printing equipment, which is far more relevant to the target audience in your micro-niche.

As market leader, you are likely to have credibility, authority and, if you are operating in a highly profitable segment, command a price premium over and above that of your competitors.

If I was to ask you, "Who was the first person to fly solo over the Atlantic?" you may well know that it was Charles Lindbergh. Do you know the second? The chances are that you would have no idea. Do you know the third? Even less likely to recall the name of that particular individual! However, if I rephrased the very last question: "Who was the first woman to fly solo across the Atlantic?", then you'd be right in saying Amelia Earhart, the third person - but the first woman.

Considering your core competencies and redefining your space should be one of the first places to look for differential advantage.

So, the first law, according to Reis and Trout, is: "It's better to be first than it is to be better." The second law is: "If you can't be first in a category, then set up a category that you can be first in."

Case Study - 'Genuine Pioneers'

"We are the pioneers of the world; the advance-guard, sent on through the wilderness of untried things, to break a new path in the New World..."

Herman Melville

"Once an organization loses its spirit of pioneering and rests on its early work, its progress stops."

Thomas J. Watson

Brief: To establish the core brand essence and sources of competitive advantage. To focus on the company's leadership positioning within the environmental due diligence and reporting market across every media platform.

Solution: Strand Financial conducted a brand workshop with key management and employees and developed the positioning platform of 'Genuine Pioneers', highlighting GroundSure's standing as the first supplier of environmental due diligence reports to provide expert interpretation.

Core Brand Essence

Genuine

adj

1. *Real – having the qualities or value claimed*

2. *Sincere – not affected or pretended*

3. *Honest – open in relationships with others*

Pioneers

n

1. *A person or group that is the first to do something in a specified field*

2. *A forerunner in creating, exploring and developing something new*

3. *Somebody who goes into previously uncharted or unclaimed territory with the purpose of exploring it and possibly owning it*

Brand Pillars

For your brand to be successful there needs to be intellectual and emotional alignment with your target audiences. Brand pillars are those vital factors (usually expressed as three distinct qualities) that support the core essence of your business.

Exercise 14 – Building Brand Pillars

Look at the words you wrote down originally and pick the ones of greatest relevance and support to the core essence you have selected.

For your brand to be successful there needs to be a strong intellectual and emotional alignment with your target audiences, so try to make sure that at least two of the three contain an evocative benefit.

Exercise 15 – Ask the Thesaurus

Taking your core essence and each of your brand pillars, look up these words in a Thesaurus.

Write down positive associations that you feel would build your brand vocabulary.

Choose the most evocative words that are most likely to achieve an emotional response.

Expand these into sentences showing how you describe your business. Refine them and you will now be able to talk about your business in a way that lights you up and your customers.

Speed, strength and flexibility

Brief: To develop a corporate identity that maps to the brand pillars of SME Invoice Finance, which is dedicated to the values demanded by cash hungry small businesses, all the more relevant in times of economic uncertainty.

Solution: Strand Financial has developed a strongly differentiated icon for SME Invoice Finance, the 'Big Cat,' that represents the key attributes that the fast-growth owner managed sector demands, namely speed, strength and flexibility. The striking use of purple has been adopted as an integral part of the corporate color palette, making the 'Big Cat' icon stand out from the crowd. The result is an instantly recognizable corporate image with a distinctive personality of its own. This dedication to meeting the needs of the owner managed business sector underpins the entire business model.

"The Virgin brand promise is based on five key factors: value for money, quality, reliability, innovation and an indefinable, but nonetheless palpable, sense of fun."

Richard Branson

Your brand vocabulary

It's time to Light Your Firebrand by using language more innovatively. The way in which to achieve a differentiated position, as you will discover, is to develop your core essence, brand pillars, elevator pitch and unique value propositions (UVPs). This can only be pulled through to engagement once you have your own brand thesaurus, a unified language set, to be applied by everyone across the entire organization from reception to C-level.

For a brand to become successful, the brand thesaurus does not start and finish with the ubiquitous press release or marketing collateral but must be cascaded into every business conversation - internally and externally.

Discovering your Unique Value Propositions

Ralph Waldo Emerson has been quoted as saying, "What you do speaks so loud that I cannot hear what you say." It would be fair to say that many service organizations focus simply on the product benefits level, which is unlikely to be a differentiator unless it impacts on service. The difference between companies is therefore not so much 'what you do' but 'who you are' and 'how you do your business differently.'

Rosser Reeves coined the phrase USP as an acronym for the Unique Selling Proposition in the 1950s, when features based advertising was the norm. Today, the term USP is used casually, predominantly by non-marketers, to describe or focus on any differentiated attribute.

It is not over-rated, simply out-moded as a marketing concept. Today, rather than having a single USP, sustainable differentiation comes through redefining or 're-imagining' the customer experience based on your core essence – a development we call the UVPs - Unique Value Propositions.

These are the specific, tangible actions or service-related benefits you will deliver to your customers as a result of introducing your new core essence.

Unique Value Propositions are therefore:

The intrinsic values that a brand provides to its customers or constituents over other alternatives.

The functional, emotional, and self-expressive benefits that provide value to the customer and provide the rationale for making one brand choice over another.

I told this story at Communicate Magazine's Reputation in Financial Services Conference, about a sports team that was barely keeping itself afloat. You really couldn't eat the burgers at the ground, wouldn't want to go to the restroom and the game wasn't any more enjoyable than either. Gate receipts were going down. You get the picture. The CEO changed the team's fortunes by making one decision – the smartest decision he could ever have made – by putting the core essence, 'great family entertainment,' right at the center of their dial. Imagine this as a result – great burgers, bands at half time, clean restrooms you could change a baby in, fireworks after games. You know what, they started winning games and players were inundated with requests for autographs – all from having a clear vision articulating their UVPs.

Once you have established your unique value propositions, differentiation becomes part of your marketing strategy and allows you to take a leadership position in the marketplace.

The only constant in business is change. Your UVPs are not static slogans on a piece of paper tacked to your wall. The value you bring to the market must change and evolve as the market shifts. Whilst your core essence remains a constant, it is important to adjust your UVPs to remain in tune with the needs of your prospects and clients. Make a point to evaluate and adjust your differentiation approach at least annually.

Exercise 16 – What are your UVPs?

Draw a small diamond in the middle of a piece of paper and write down your core essence.

Now place eight small circles around it - connected to the diamond with straight lines.

Brainstorm tangible aspects of your service delivery, based on your core essence and complete your 'circle satellite'.

As a result of this exercise, you will have a fresh set of powerful Unique Value Propositions!

SMART UVPs

GroundSure used SMART Objectives (specific, measurable, attainable, relevant and timebound) in order to 'live' its innovative UVPs as Genuine Pioneers:

- Launched the first added-value expertly interpreted residential environmental report

- The first company in its sector to introduce an expert helpline in support of its reports

- The first to produce a report designed specifically for the end-user and to incorporate design elements such as an aerial photograph and clear signposting

- Radically altered the price point for commercial due diligence environmental reports

- Developed and launched Siteguard, a ground-breaking desktop report for environmental due diligence, which includes a unique feature – an automatic insurance quote

- The web site we designed won the prestigious and coveted British Computer Society Award for Innovation

"GroundSure Limited was set up as a provider of environmental reports for property transactions. We were entering a market with two established competitors in an industry with a complicated route to market and entrenched supplier and distributor channels. As Marketing Director, I knew I needed a dramatically different and powerful brand to gain awareness, credibility, and customers. GroundSure was sold just 6 years later for £44 million to EMAP and that level of success would not have been possible without the skills of Mike Symes and John Dillon."

Jaynie Macdonald

The Name in the Flames

The name game

"A brand name is more than a word. It is the beginning of a conversation."

Lexicon

I love this story from Alan Fletcher. It goes something like this:

A lady, sitting next to Raymond Loewy at dinner, struck up a conversation.

"Why," she asked, "did you put two Xs in Exxon?"

"Why ask?" he replied.

"Because," she said, "I couldn't help noticing."

"Well," he responded, "That's the answer."

There's a great deal more to brand naming than adding an additional X, but I hope you get the spirit of what I'm trying to say here.

Never in the history of marketing, branding, advertising or design has the name game been more important or more difficult. This is a step-by-step guide to the name game.

Descriptive

Descriptive names are exactly that – existing words with obvious meanings or associations. Descriptive names normally ascribe to the company or product a characteristic, feature, ingredient, appearance or geographic location. Examples of descriptive product names include British Airways, American Airlines, Shredded Wheat, Philadelphia Cream Cheese and Florida Orange Juice.

Associative

These are actual words related to the core essence/ unique value proposition, allowing for more evocative association. These tend to be visually strong in terms of direction, frequently drawing on metaphor as a source of inspiration. Visa (evokes travel rather than financial borrowings), Southern Comfort (a smooth and mellow experience), O2 (a breath of fresh air).

Invented

These are made up words that sound appealing and may consist of Latin, Greek and other languages. Long-established examples include Kodak, Xerox and Coca-Cola. Think of some of the Web 2.0 business names: YouTube, TechCrunch, Squidoo, Gizmodo. Those words did not exist until they were invented. They are 'meaningfully coined', distinctive and usually easy to remember.

Arbitrary

A real name with little or no immediate connection with the brand's position in the market. These are real words, but used differently from their ordinary meaning. Apple, for example, was created because Steve Jobs worked on an apple farm and also believed apples to be the perfect fruit!

Eponymous

These bear the name, initials or fragment of the owner or parent company name and hint at personal levels of service, stewardship and care. Many of these names are concentrated in such sectors as finance (Merrill Lynch, Morgan Stanley, Goldman Sachs) and fashion (Louis Vuitton, Gucci, Chanel), but they are to be found in most industries, as Mercedes-Benz, Gillette, Kellogg's, Pfizer, Harley-Davidson, Wrigley's, Hertz, and Heineken show.

Exercise 17 – Namestorming

A great name is the mark of a great brand.

This Namestorming exercise follows a five stage sequence, designed to generate a substantial number of potential names at the speed of thought:

Exploratory Rapid freestyle creative brainstorm based on core essence and brand pillars

Company attributes focused brainstorm UVPs

Product / services Based on product and service process, customer experience and characteristics

Researched brainstorm Web based research

Associative brainstorm Use the collective pool of words and phrases to spark new concepts adding previously unconnected words, prefixes and suffixes together to create new meanings

The Filter Matrix

Having created a pool of 50 to 100 potential brand names, the next stage is to apply some negative filters. This model has been designed to replicate the responses of a (cynical) target audience.

Quickly apply these reactions to your names using the Filter Matrix and you will see how and why some names will not make it through to the positive scoring phase.

"So what?" (bland or too generic)

"Heard it all before." (me-too, hackneyed)

"Oh yeah??" (unbelievable, an advertising puff)

"Yeah, right." (prompts a sarcastic or negative response)

"Eh?" (style over substance, pretentious, contrived or abstract)

"Yawn." (tedious, meaningless corporate waffle, over-complicated, clumsy)

Simply remove any names that score two or more negative comments.

Don't become overly concerned that so many names are falling by the wayside or that you feel you are keeping so many in. Ultimately, all you are looking for is one name at the conclusion of the entire process!

By the end of this exercise, you should have around 20 potential brand names left.

Exercise 18a – The Filter Matrix

Apply all potential names to the Filter Matrix

BRANDSTORMING FILTERS	Name 1	Name 2	Name 3	Name 4	Name 5
"So what?" (bland or too generic)					
"Heard it all before." (me-too, hackneyed)					
"Oh yeah??" (unbelievable, an advertising puff)					
"Yeah, right." (prompts a sarcastic or negative response)					
"Eh?" (style over substance, pretentious, contrived or abstract)					
"Yawn." (tedious, meaningless corporate waffle, over-complicated, clumsy)					

Exercise 18b – The Taxonomy Table

Map 'Passed' Names to Taxonomy Chart

NAME DEVELOPMENT SCORING MODEL	YES	NO	N/A
Distinctive			
Memorable			
Simple			
Campaignable			
Appearance			
Sound			
Energy / Buzz			
Depth / Layers of Meaning			
Humanity			
Maps to Key Messages			
Maps to Core Values			
Maps to Competitive Edge			
Trademark (ability)			
Domain Availability			

Scoring

This is the fun part. Score the remaining names by applying the 14 criteria set out in the Taxonomy Table.

Score one point for each of the positive criteria you have ticked.

Then, count up the scores and take the 10 highest ranking names.

With the help of an online thesaurus or dictionary, copy and paste the definitions associated with these names onto a document

Present your top 5 names and edited definitions to the group

(A word about domain names. Although obviously desirable, do not be disappointed if at first you are unable to obtain the domain name of your choice in .com or .co.uk form.

You can try adding a suffix, such as 'online' or a description of your micro-niche, using a hyphen between words or consider a .net extension.)

"What's in a name? That which we call a rose by any other word would smell as sweet."

William Shakespeare - Romeo and Juliet (II, ii, 1-2)

Naming Case Studies

Cerno Capital

Brief: Independent Wealth Management wanted to change its name, as the brand name used by the firm also belonged to its sister company in Geneva.

Solution: A brand workshop conducted by Strand Financial with the managing partners at Independent Wealth Management identified that being highly selective is at the heart of the proposition, which centers on seeking out talented, experienced fund managers. Strand Financial distilled the core essence of the brand into a single word, 'select.' The next step was to create a brand name and corporate identity that maps exactly to the core essence. Following a comprehensive brand naming process, based on proven, proprietary filter matrices, Strand Financial recommended 'Cerno Capital'. 'Cerno' is Latin for 'select' and the root of the English word 'discerning.' A classic seraph font in a deep corporate blue conveys the gravitas and authority inherent within the brand. The brand pillars are talent, transparency and trust.

'OSMO'

Brief: To create a product brand name and identity for the market-leading customer financial data transfer specialist, Vision Critical, to reach the next level - becoming recognized as a truly global software brand.

Solution: The two 'cells' in different shades of blue, combined with the flowing logo symbolize the dynamic process of data exchange. The product identity and character, OSMO® (a morpheme or contracted form of the biological term, 'osmosis') was developed to evoke the real-time transfer, absorption and equalisation of data with 'effortless transparency.'

The Quartz Partnership

Brief: Receivables Management Services specialist, Bradbury Financial Limited, appointed Strand Financial to create a new brand name and corporate identity. The decision to re-brand is a reflection of the company's growth and ambition to become widely recognized as an international, best-in-class business.

Solution: Following a detailed brand naming process, Strand Financial rebranded Bradbury Financial Limited as The Quartz Partnership, underlining the clarity, precision and strength of the business offering. The corporate identity features a crystal globe with clasped hands, illustrating the growing international nature of the projects being handled by the firm and the close working relationships that The Quartz Partnership enjoys with its clients. The re-brand has received a superb response from clients, prospects and industry professionals since its launch.

Litmus Advisory

Brief: To re-brand Postern Advisory and develop a new corporate identity that reflects the company's vision and re-affirms its market position as a leading debt advisory firm to its key stakeholders.

Solution: The re-brand from Postern Advisory to Litmus Advisory was far more than a new name or logo. Above all, the new brand represents the company's exclusive focus on delivering certainty of outcome for transactions in the asset based lending market. Strand Financial's proprietary brand model was used to score, filter and prioritize the new brand name. The use of litmus paper colors creates a strong visual identity that underlines the rigorous nature of the due diligence process. In these tough times, delivering certainty is a vital message.

'Delivering'

- To do what has been promised
- To provide or produce something
- To save somebody from captivity or hardship
- To hand something or somebody over to someone else
- To deliver new life, i.e. birth

'Certainty'

- A conclusion or outcome that is beyond doubt
- Definitely known, fixed or settled
- Able to be relied upon
- Somebody who is strongly expected to win
- A complete lack of doubt about something

Mark My Words

The primary purpose of a registered trademark is to prevent people from becoming confused about the source or origin of a service and to help people answer the question: "Who provides this service?"

As people become familiar with the services your brand represents, it will acquire a secondary meaning as an indicator of quality and help people answer another question: "Can I expect a good service?" For this reason, your trademark is an important asset, which should be protected.

Trademark law protects marks. Marks can be words, names, symbols or devices. They come in several classes:

Trademark

A trademark is a mark that distinguishes one person's goods from others'. In practice, the word "trademark" is often used to refer to any class of mark that is protected under trademark law.

Service mark A service mark is similar to a trademark, except that it is used to distinguish one person's services from others'. Service marks can be registered in the same manner as trademarks and are denoted by the ® symbol once they are registered on the appropriate registers. If they are not registered, they often carry an SM symbol.

Trade name A trade name is a mark used to identify a business, as opposed to a product or service.

Certification mark A certification mark is a mark used to certify a product in some way, regardless of its specific source. Seals of approval (e.g. the Good Housekeeping Seal of Approval) and marks of origin (e.g. Roquefort cheese) are examples of certification marks. A certification mark is held by an organization and is protected under trademark law so long as the holder establishes a standard for awarding the mark and polices that standard effectively.

Collective mark A collective mark is a mark held by a group for the use of its members. Examples include union stamps and franchise marks.

Brand architecture

Brand architecture is seen traditionally as how a company structures and names its brand and how all the brand names relate to each other.

Architecture is a critical component for establishing strategic relationships and there are three types that have been categorized:

1. Monolithic, where all products and services bear the corporate brand name (also known as masterbrand strategy).

2. Freestanding, where each product or service is individually branded for its target market and the corporate brand operates as a holding company.

3. Endorsed, where all sub-brands are linked to the corporate brand either verbally or visually.

Over the years, we have seen multiple variations of these company structures. The fundamentals of good architecture remain the same – that the client always remains at the heart of the architectural decision-making process.

However, there is a potentially difficult issue that needs to be confronted here. Should there be a wish at any time for the sale of one part of the business, common product brand name ownership or strapline would inevitably become an issue. Therefore all matters of brand architecture need to be considered with extreme care.

Spark Chapter Challenge

In striking our sparks, we have:

1. Identified key attributes for which we can potentially command a leadership position.

2. Distilled our brand down to one or two key words that we want to 'own' in our customers' minds – our core essence.

3. Engineered / re-engineered our unique value propositions around our core essence to provide meaning for our customers.

4. Identified clearly defined brand pillars (the guiding insights and qualities that support the essence of our brand).

5. Created a brand vocabulary for all employees that maps directly to the core essence of our brand.

Step 3 - Flame

"Sometimes our light goes out but is blown into flame by another human being. Each of us owes deepest thanks to those who have rekindled this light."

Albert Schweitzer

Flame on!

"When you discover your mission, you will feel its demand. It will fill you with enthusiasm and a burning desire to get to work on it."

W. Clement Stone

A few years ago, I went to the Red Bull Air Race with my youngest son. Seconds before the single seater planes burst forwards over the sparkling water, the official announcement, 'Flame on', cut through as a go-signal heralding a spectacular aerodynamic display of breathtaking speed, agility and split-second timing. Is your 'flame on', when you are asked to pitch?

Elevate your messages

You're in an elevator. The CEO of your hottest prospect is also in the elevator and recognizes you. He says, "I'm curious, tell me what you do again?" You're at a networking event. You just happen to run into a key person of influence in an industry you know well. "Great to meet you. I've seen you at these events before but haven't got round to speaking to you. Tell me some more about yourself!"

Why is it that so many senior executives struggle when they are asked to say what they do in typical situations such as those described above? They are experts in their field of business, yet they clam up or say something that simply is not going to be distinctive enough to be memorable. Do you think that they have their 'flame on?'

The only way to avoid those missed opportunities is to have a carefully crafted 30-second elevator speech ready and waiting.

Imagine that what you are doing is like writing a trailer for a movie blockbuster - it has to grab your attention and make you excited enough to want to learn more. Here is one very famous example of the elevator pitch trailer:

"Space, the final frontier.

These are the voyages of the starship Enterprise.

Its five-year mission: to explore strange new worlds... to seek out new life... and new civilizations...

To boldly go where no man has gone before!"

Exercise 19 – The Power Pitch

Answer the following questions and you are well on the way to creating a memorable and compelling elevator pitch that will set you apart from the crowd and win you more and better business. It answers four basic questions, and it invites the listener to say, "Tell me more."

Question 1: What does your company do that's different to your competitors? (Remarkable)

Question 2: Who does your company do it for? (Reputational)

Question 3: What problem do I solve? (Relevant)

Question 4: Why do they care? Or, what's in it for them? (Real)

"Only [brand] delivers [Q1] to the [target] market, working with companies such as [Q2] to [Q3], which enables them to [Q4]."

It's far more than a mission statement, it's understanding your business in a way that gets people excited, involved, and thinking.

The most audacious pitch of all time

I was having lunch with a PR friend of mine last week, who reminded me of what must amount to the most audacious pitch of all time. So the story goes, an advertising agency was invited to pitch for the British Rail account, as it had just come up for tender. The incumbent agency was expected to win and the agency quoted here was something of a 'wildcard' inclusion.

When the BR team arrived at the agency, they did not receive the customary polite greeting. Instead, they were met by a disinterested receptionist sitting at her desk, filing her nails and smoking a cigarette. She then made the entire executive team wait until she had finished reading the newspaper, before pointing them dismissively in the direction of a waiting room that was full of dirty cups and rubbish. The tea provided was undrinkable.

As legend has it, they were made to wait for at least twenty minutes and just as they got up to leave, the ad agency MD came in bold as brass and said: "This is how your customers perceive British Rail's service. We intend to change that for you." They then opened the doors of the boardroom to reveal their vision of the future of BR. The agency was hired immediately and started work that week.

George Bernard Shaw once said: "The reasonable man adapts himself to the conditions that surround him... The unreasonable man adapts surrounding conditions to himself... All progress depends on the unreasonable man."

Once again, the unreasonable, disruptive and bold move won the day. Some might call it high risk; the biggest risk would have been to play it safe!

Telling Your Fire Story

"When a heart is on fire, sparks always fly out of the mouth."

Proverb

Since early cave dwellers left their graffiti in Lascaux, we have relied on storytelling to define who we are. Stories help people learn, absorb, remember and share information and ideas. They have the power to motivate, persuade and inspire, leading to direct collective action.

Compelling stories have far-reaching emotional impact and form a powerful currency in human relationships as they are told and re-told. It makes no sense whatsoever to me that the original and most powerful form of communication and learning – storytelling – does not have a greater place in the world of business today.

The *Cluetrain Manifesto*, a set of 95 theses drawn up as a call to action for every business, states: "Stories are much more compelling than information. Stories differ from information in that they have a start and a finish; they talk about events, not conditions; they imply a deep relationship among the events; stories are about particular humans; and stories are told in a human voice. As markets once again become conversations, marketers need to excel at telling compelling stories."

In an age where social networking is bringing individuals and communities together and where we need to engage increasingly at an emotional level, marketers need to re-learn the art of storytelling.

This is the age of the brand-bite, the era of the authentic brand story. In these days of similar companies with 'me-too' messages, authentic brand stories are our strongest differentiator.

"Brands are built around stories, and stories of identity – who we are, where we've come from – are the most effective stories of all. This is a powerful way to bring them to life."

Bill Dauphinais
PricewaterhouseCoopers

Once upon a brand

"Nothing else worked. Charts left listeners bemused. Prose remained unread. Dialogue was just too laborious and slow." Stephen Denning was working as a director at World Bank when he discovered that every time he tried to talk to the board about investing in knowledge management armed with bullet points and spreadsheets, their eyes glazed over.

"Let me tell you something that happened two weeks ago." Denning discovered his moment of truth as he told the simple story of how one doctor in a village in Zambia could treat malaria by going online to find answers. In that defining moment, his story persuaded senior board members to invest time and money in knowledge sharing, resulting in the World Bank becoming a global leader in this area.

His corporate story changed the face of the business he worked in and saved countless lives. What could your brand story do?

Think of the process as preparing for an interview.

The brand story interview preparation:

- What was the original vision of the company?
- What is the big idea behind your product or service?
- How was the company started?
- Has your focus changed since the company was founded?
- What is your vision for the future?
- Who were the company's founding fathers / mothers?
- What was the guiding entrepreneurial philosophy?
- Is there an industry guru / technical genius behind your vision?
- What does your product or service do for your target audience?

Does your vision rely on the uniqueness of your:

a. Products

b. Services

c. Knowledge

d. Delivery system

Exercise 20 – The Lead Story

Imagine the editor of the *Financial Times* or the *Wall Street Journal* was to tell you that he or she is going to interview you this afternoon and that it will appear as the lead story. What would that story look like? Are you sitting comfortably?

Use the process to tell your story anecdotally with a clear beginning, middle and end:

1. Beginning – What made you start / join the business? What was the vision? Who were the founders?

2. Middle – Who are the characters / heroes? What is the plot? What are your values and beliefs? What are your customers' stories? Is there a twist to the tale – has your focus changed?

3. End – What is the outcome expressed in customers' / stakeholders' terms? What is the defining moment of the story? What is your vision for the future? What is the impact or outcome of your actions?

The result is your authentic brand story that you can tell with passion and belief because you were there. Now, listen carefully as your story becomes my story, becomes our story. For this is how all of the great and truly memorable corporate legends are made.

Philosophically speaking

Over the years, the media has subjected us to some amazing mixed metaphor howlers amongst the doom and gloom. We've observed credit card insurance described as "the elephant in the room, marketed by snake oil salesmen!" We were once even treated to the Large Hadron Collider acting "Like a thief in the night, sending a beam of light smaller than the width of a human hair at the speed of a jumbo jet."

Recently, newspapers have been awash with some of the most stunning oxymorons, what with talk of 'crisis management', 'tentative decisions' and 'unbiased opinions, not to mention that old staple, the 'Great Depression.' 'Government intelligence' hasn't exactly led me to be 'hopelessly optimistic' regarding the 'current history' of 'virtually identical' banks either.

In this age of the sound bite, it's helpful to get back to what clarity of communication is all about, by taking a leaf out of what is a very large book indeed - Aristotle's *Rhetoric.* If you think it's all Greek to you, here are some highlights:

1. Teleology - A Sense of Purpose Teleology (Greek: telos: end, purpose) is summed up by the ancient Greek philosopher as follows: "First, have a definite, clear practical ideal: a goal, an objective. Second, have the necessary means to achieve your ends: wisdom, money, materials, and methods. Third, adjust all your means to that end." Always relate your communication to your purpose. Never, ever lose sight of that. It sounds obvious but I seldom see it applied consistently.

2. Ethos - Become <u>the</u> Authority Ethos is authority and credibility personified - achieved by the cultivation of a distinctive character, knowledge and experience.

3. Pathos - Engage the Emotions Pathos describes what's in it for your audience, with a set of compelling benefits, values and beliefs.

4. Logos – Use Proof Points Logos means applying relevant facts and figures to support your case. Use the three modes of rhetoric, Ethos, Pathos and Logos, together for maximum effect.

5. Structure Your Story Here's Aristotle's six-step guide to writing compelling, captivating copy and powerful presentations (subject to considerable poetic license):

Exordium – Big Intro

Follow up a bold statement with a big intro that captures your target audiences' attention and imagination. Mix ethos with logos to establish credibility.

Narratio – Empathy

Show the audience you really identify with them and that you feel their pain.

Partitio – Contents

Outline to your audience what you're just about to tell them in a way that heightens anticipation and helps them remember the key points.

Confirmatio – The Solution

Outline your solution. Use case studies featuring similar organizations or demographics to that of your audience, together with facts to support your case.

Refutatio – Competitive Advantage

Take the opportunity to position the strengths of your organization, based on key attributes where your competitors are weakest.

Peroratio – Call to Action

After a headline summary of your business case, use a strong call to action to close, with the emphasis on keeping a strong emotional appeal.

Think Ansoff, Covey, Kotler, Levitt, Mintzberg and Porter, rolled into one brilliantly be-robed and bearded package. Aristotle still has a lot to teach us brand marketers.

Mind your language

The language used in marketing communications can make a vast difference to their effectiveness. Here are the major points to remember:

1. 'You, you, you' not 'we, we, we'

Talk about 'us' and 'we' and you run the risk of alienating your audience. Clients want to feel as if you are doing things just for them - after all they are concerned with their wants and needs. Make them feel important and you'll encourage them to read on.

2. Rapid results

Clients and prospects demand fast results, rapid delivery, and fast-track ordering processes. Since time is such a scarce resource today, many people value it above money. Customers will often expect results by yesterday; the use words such as 'immediate,' 'fast' and 'quick' taps into this.

3. Exclusivity

All customers want to feel special and exclusivity says something about the buyer's desire to own or receive things that are valuable or rare. Feed your customers' sense of importance by offering them something that isn't available to everyone.

4. Easy

Clients want to make things as simple and convenient as possible. They want to be able to order, purchase and use your products or services with genuine ease. Make the process as easy as possible. Assure prospective customers that buying your service will involve them in the minimum of effort.

5. No risk

Customers need to feel confident about the deal. Use words such as 'secure,' 'assured,' 'certainty' and 'reliability' to minimize the risk factor.

6. Complimentary

Offer free products and services to give that extra incentive to act.

7. Discount / special offer

Everyone loves a bargain. They could be sales, percentage discounts, 'get one free' offers.

8. Guaranteed

Certainty and reliability are powerful drivers in convincing customers to buy, handling the 'risk objection'. However, guaranteed has to be the ultimate in confident, re-assuring statements. Make sure you can back it up in terms of service and legality.

9. Important

It's human nature to stop and take notice of important instructions. No one wants to make a mistake or miss out on vital information that will affect their lives. Make the customer feel that they'll be missing out on crucial information if they don't read your communication.

10. Innovative

Nothing fires the imagination as much as something new. The latest information technology appeals to the 'early adopter'. Make sure your product stands out as new and interesting, rather than the 'same old, same old'.

Today, I'm going to **save you** time and **money** by giving you **exclusive** information about an **important, complimentary new** report into the proven power words. These top ten words are **guaranteed** to improve the **results** of your marketing and it's so **easy** to apply them to make your campaigns even more **innovative** and **secure** in the knowledge that your business will thrive.

Time for tone – an extract from the Fidelity style guide

The way we say things is just as important as what we say. This excellent example of a concise style guide from Fidelity demonstrates a real commitment to employing the correct tone of voice.

"Fidelity aims to achieve a tone of voice that conveys and reinforces our core brand values. Our voice should be a human one - real, friendly and informative, presenting the company as committed, professional and trustworthy."

Fidelity's copy objectives

"Customer-focused: know who you are talking to and adapt the tone and content accordingly.

Benefits-focused: concentrate on the benefits to the customer, not the features of the product or service.

Clear: however long you've been working in the investment arena, keep trying to put yourselves into your clients' shoes. Will they understand easily, or is the copy heavy with financial services jargon? If you must use jargon, explain it in plain terms immediately.

Competent: use an authoritative tone, to help position Fidelity as an expert and the market leader. The tone of voice should show how seriously we take our jobs, recognizing that customers have put their trust in us and demonstrating how we live up to that trust. However, confidence should not be pushed into arrogance.

Concise: get your point across as soon as you can, or you might lose your readers halfway through your text.

Humor: this is useful in the financial arena and has been used to great effect by Fidelity. But it has to be the right kind of humor. We don't want: flip, frivolous, puns and gags. We do want: apposite wit, bon mots. It's not about raising a laugh just to get a laugh - it's about raising a laugh, or even just a wry smile, to make a point.

Personal / accessible: avoid formal, old-fashioned language. As a test, read your copy out loud and see how it sounds. But take care not to go the other way - too chatty or clever and you could sound patronizing and as if you're talking down to our clients. The use of humor or irony can help us to communicate on the readers' wavelength.

Accurate: check your work carefully. Typographical and grammatical errors detract from the overall quality of our material."

I really enjoyed this blog from the *Copywriter's Crucible*:

"Standing out from the crowd is difficult in any marketplace. One of the ways they (Innocent) differentiated themselves, from all the other brightly colored labels, was through their copywriting. Their copy presents them as fun, quirky and witty. They were the plucky upstarts taking on the big corporate brands, with a new approach to business, and people loved it."

Innocent drinks now dominate the UK smoothie market, and it's in no small part due to the personality of their copywriting.

Be heroic

We live in the world of the sound bite. Yet, how can politicians on both sides of the pond have got the positioning of their role in the banking crisis so very wrong?

It doesn't take much to work out that the word 'bailout' has negative connotations. It smacks of disaster, of failure – and no one takes to that positioning.

I agree wholeheartedly with our clients Euro RSCG who said, "What if this had been called a 'rescue' from the beginning? Or the 'Save our Homes Act?' Supporting a 'rescue' is a bear of an entirely different species. It is not only a redemptive act, restoring things to their rightful order - it is heroic. Today consumers choose brands that share their values. Supporting a rescue says something important about our values and our personal character to those around us. It says I care. It says I am a good person. It says I am a hero too."

Inspiring image

'The visual image is a kind of tripwire for the emotions.'

Diane Ackerman

A brand must communicate what it stands for using as few words / images as possible, so keep the message simple but memorable.

A visual difference is important for four reasons:

1. It gets your brand noticed in a crowded marketplace

2. It establishes your unique position

3. It reminds customers of your brand every time they see your visual difference

4. It creates an emotional connection

Effective execution

Image alone can help differentiate a commodity - whether based on real or perceived benefits - as long as the strategy is executed properly. Images can be built to inform customers about hidden or small differences that they might otherwise be unaware of and thus turn these differences into something that, in their own minds, they simply cannot live without.

Maintaining adherence to clear brand standards

Be consistent in terms of the look and feel of your brand. Inconsistency leads to the dilution of awareness and message retention. If you don't think you can commit to this, look deeper..Maybe it's time to refresh your corporate identity or image before you drive forward with your planned regular communications. If you're proud of your brand you will want to see it out there all the time.

Flame Proof

Proof points

Have your brand take a lead over the bland. Focus on the numbers that really matter - the proof points you must have to back up every differentiating claim you make about your products and services. Such as the number of years clients stay with your firm and the percentage of clients that refer you new business opportunities.

Identify some supporting logical or factual proof for your differentiation statement. The stronger the proof, the more believable the differentiation statement is. And the more believable it is, the greater its impact in generating customer awareness and sales. One caveat: do make sure that your proof points are superior to those of your competitors!

The key is to have several layers of ammunition to prove your business's worth to a potential client and to make your product or service stand above that of the competition. It is vital that these proof points are validated and I would like to use one of Strand Financial's clients, Vision Critical, to illustrate my point.

In the *Business Money Annual Review*, Editor Bob Lefroy comments: "It was a master stroke (Close Invoice Finance) being first to the party with the revolutionary IDeal discounting product, one that makes use of Vision Critical's real time reconciliation systems. It allows greater exposure levels with much lower administration costs making the product a ferocious competitor in terms of flexibility, cost and service.

The figures reflect this. Factoring business is down over-all but just look at the discounting numbers with sales and advances up 31% and client numbers up 25%. Average loan size is up 5%, operational efficiency measured by the client/officer ratio has improved 50% in five years."

This contained a wide range of proof points. Within the space of a few paragraphs, we learn that:

1. Vision Critical works with BLUE-CHIP CLIENTS, such as Close Invoice Finance.

2. The level of third-party ENDORSEMENT is two-fold, that of the respected editor of the leading industry trade magazine and that of the CEO of Close Invoice Finance.

3. The IDeal product was FIRST to market with Vision Critical's innovative technology.

4. An aggressive MARKET LEADERSHIP position established by messaging such as 'master stroke,' 'first to the party' and 'ferocious competitor.'

5. The client demonstrates SUPERIOR TECH-NOLOGICAL ADVANTAGE, as evidenced by the 'revolutionary' product reference (n.b. this approach can also be applied to patents, unique processes, industry secrets and guarantees).

6. The entire proposition is supported by HARD FACTS, unequivocal evidence of customer advantage - 'sales and advances up 31%,' 'client numbers up 25%,' 'Average loan size is up 5%,' 'operational efficiency measured by the client/officer ratio has improved 50%.'

7. There has been sustainable improvement demonstrated by BEFORE AND AFTER COMPARISONS - 'improved 50% in 5 years.'

Exercise 21 – Bulletproof your brand

Question 1: What does your company do that's different to your competitors?

e.g. We are the world's largest fork lift truck leasing company with £x million being advanced.

Question 2: For whom does your company do it?

e.g. Our service is used by 87 of the Fortune 100.

Question 3: What problem do I solve?

e.g. We have leased 85% of the top 10 manufacturers' trucks, so we understand the asset better than anyone and offer a 55% higher acceptance rate.

Question 4: What benefits do our clients get?

e.g. An easier process, with 98% of clients signing up for leases on additional equipment.

Spreading Messages Like Wildfire

"Bright-flaming, heat-full fire,
the source of motion."

Du Bartas

Stand for something – and make it inspiring

TRUE Creativity and Innovation consists of

SEEING what everyone else has seen,

THINKING what no one else has thought, and

DOING what no one else has dared!

Big ideas break rules. Shatter conventions. Challenge the status quo.

What characterizes them is their total and uncompromising shift away from what has gone before. They smash through the entire safe, culturally embedded biases and conventions that shape standard approaches to business thinking. A big idea must be pursued with conviction, passion, courage, credibility, tenacity and decisiveness. Sounds exciting? It is.

You know what is even more exciting? By following the Light Your Firebrand™ process, you already have your big idea. An animating big idea. An inspiring big idea. A compelling big idea.

It's the core essence of your brand.

Conventional wisdom says the secret to great marketing communications is to develop a big idea for a campaign. A Firebrand marketer develops a campaign for a big idea. Mere semantics – not at all.

Apple's big idea is innovation. Intel's big idea is performance. GE's big idea is imagination.

One look at the messages on GE's web site leaves you in no doubt as to the core essence of their brand and their big idea. "GE is imagination at work. From jet engines to power generation, financial services to water processing, and medical imaging to media content, GE people worldwide are dedicated to turning imaginative ideas into leading products and services that help solve some of the world's toughest problems."

The messages build upon the big idea as we explore the web site further and deepen our involvement: "Is it possible to change the world? At GE we are doing it one idea at a time."

"For GE, imagination at work is more than a slogan or a tagline," CEO Jeff Immelt says on the site. "It is a reason for being."

Firebrand marketers understand that, as valuable as their products and services are, they are often transient in nature. Brands, however, live on in the hearts and minds of customers. Celebrate your 'reason for being' through messages that are rooted in the core idea that ignites your company. Then spark new messages that will light up your customers, leaving them feeling inspired.

There are three vital elements concerned with creating breakthrough ideas.

The wave of messages you develop can create a deep and lasting impact, challenging Market Standards, generating Market Shift and resulting in Market Space.

Market Standards

Market Standards are those conventions that we don't even notice because they are so familiar. It's those ready-made ideas that maintain the status quo.

T. S. Eliot said, "It's not wise to violate rules until you know how to observe them." Successfully smashing standards requires one or more of the following: knowledge, power, and tolerance for risk. To understand the existing market position is important. You need to know how to play an instrument well before you can improvise. You need to know the rules intimately to know how best to break them.

Market Shift

Market Shift occurs where, all at once, we question the way we have done things in the past. We discover that our way of thinking has been conditioned by biases. However, the market shift precludes conservatism. It doesn't settle for the safe and the predictable. On the contrary, the market shift stage is about all-out questioning, about developing new hypotheses and unexpected ideas. It is a journey into uncharted territory, a quest for angles of attack that have never been used before. Market shift is the art to come up with better questions, to cross conventional boundaries and to overcome opinions and prejudices, which inhibit the creation of new possibilities and visionary ideas.

Market Space

Low-level market shifts are those that result when attacking a convention leads to a renewal of the brand, not the market. The brand's place within a given market has been shifted as opposed to the displacement of the market itself. By contrast, a high-level market shift occurs when the company, by expressing a new vision, displaces the entire market, creating a new market space - where they have room to grow - even more profitably.

The case for consistency

Base your communications on a central theme - your clear core brand essence. This is a distinctive attribute that you alone can own. Apply the truth of your supporting messages consistently and creatively across your chosen media.

Be true to your marketing strategy and see it through - don't pull marketing spend as a knee-jerk reaction. If you withdraw your marketing, what is it saying to the rest of the market and how is anyone going to notice your brand out there? Now is the time to increase your spend and take more market share, particularly if your industry is going through a period of dramatic consolidation. The real risk is standing still - in reality it will mean you are going backwards. If your competition begins holding back on their marketing spend – this is your opportunity to take their enquiries.

Communicate more regularly - issue regular email updates on products, services and successes and drive traffic to generate enquiry. Be smart with segmentation by market, job title and interest. Make sure that you gain the commitment of everyone in the organization to continue to feed you these gold nuggets of information. There's a lot less noise – and a lot more opportunity. Invest in marketing and you are guaranteed a greater share of voice. In a market in which there is an absence of data informing you of exactly when prospects plan to move to a new product or service provider, you'd better be in touch with them every month.

Be consistent - Being consistent does not mean being complacent or being static – keep your marketing fresh and creative and rotate your communications to entice your prospects.

Being consistent means delivering your brand's message in a tone that becomes recognizable as the voice of your brand. This involves communicating your brand's values and 'personality' to its target audience day after day, year after year, anywhere and everywhere! Consistency is applicable in every facet of your brand's communications strategy. Ensure your brand consistently targets its audience, communicates the same message, personifies and transmits the same values, and appears with the same vocabulary, design elements, and graphics.

Calvin Coolidge, the 30th President of the USA said, "Nothing in this world can take the place of persistence. Talent will not; nothing is more common than unsuccessful people with talent. Genius will not; unrewarded genius is almost a proverb. Education will not; the world is full of educated derelicts. Persistence and determination alone are omnipotent. The slogan 'press on' has solved and always will solve the problems of the human race."

Sure, the words 'community,' 'creativity,' 'concept' and 'campaign' sound so much more dynamic and exciting than 'consistency' but without the latter they will not flourish.

Integrated marketing

"Long-term brand equity and growth depends on our ability to successfully integrate and implement all elements of a comprehensive marketing program."

Timm F Crull, Chairman & CEO of Nestle

Exercise 22 - What's the Score?

Apply this simple scoring system to the list of marketing and communications elements to help you prioritize your integrated marketing programs.

Apply Prefix A, B or C against Suffix X, Y or Z against each item.

Obviously, high impact, low cost (AX) is the most desirable scenario. See what suits your business and your budget but never stint on quality.

Prefix A = high impact

Prefix B = medium impact

Prefix C = low impact

Suffix X = low cost

Suffix Y = medium cost

Suffix Z = high cost

Communications Checklist

Corporate identity

Stationery

(business cards, letterheads, compliments slips)

Website

Search engine optimization

Social media (LinkedIn, Facebook, Twitter)

Email templates

Brochures

Product literature

Direct mail

Presentations

Advertising

Newsletters

Events

Public relations

Videos

Exhibition stand

Telephone calls / Telemarketing

We're all for integrated marketing, we just refrain from using the words media neutral. It's simply that we don't ever want to recommend a strategy to our clients that we feel either 'neutral' or 'agnostic' about. Of course we believe in using the right media, with the right message at the right time to communicate with each customer segment - it's just that the terminology doesn't sit well with a creative agency know for its Light Your Firebrand™ philosophy.

Follow up or fade away

Do you intend to give your prospects and key business introducers away to your nearest competitors? Of course not. But you could be doing just that by not following up enough. In today's market conditions, persistence is power. Take a look at these eye-opening statistics:

48% of sales people never follow up with a prospect

25% of sales people make a second contact and stop

12% of sales people only make three contacts and stop

Factor in the following:

2% of sales are made on the first contact

3% of sales are made on the second contact

5% of sales are made on the third contact

10% of sales are made on the fourth contact

80% of sales are made on the fifth to twelfth contact

If that wasn't bad enough, just take a look at the reasons why people stop buying from businesses:

1% die, 3% move away, 5% follow a recommendation, 9% find an alternative they perceive to be better quality or value, 14% are dissatisfied with the products or services.

And a massive 68% of people leave a business because they do not feel valued.

It's time to substitute 'analysis' with 'action' and 'prevarication' with 'persistence'. Think of new ways that you can act now to follow up better. Mix media - send regular monthly direct mail and email communications in a variety of formats (but maintain your branding consistency). Keep your messages fresh. Look to inform, inspire and entertain.

Marketing messages in the recent past have been pre-occupied with the nature of the crisis and coping strategies, concerned with survival (e.g. 'cash despite the crash'). The current environment still demands a grounded approach based on TRUST and SUPPORT, yet identifies with AMBITION – a shift from 'survive' to 'thrive' (e.g. 'emerge stronger').

The following themes have come out of a study conducted by photolibrary Getty Images, indicating current terms used by marketers and their agencies when searching for images:

Balance, connection, dedication, dreams, excellence, expertise, future, goals, growth, guidance, innovation, integrity, journey, leadership, nurturing, partnership, reliability, responsive, service, teamwork, togetherness, trust, vision, winning.

Viral combustion

In *The Tipping Point,* Malcolm Gladwell says, "Simply by finding and reaching those few special people who hold so much social power, we can shape the course of social epidemics...Look at the world around you...With the slightest push – in the right place – it can be tipped."

The reality is that your existing customers make the most powerful brand evangelists, for testimonials, co-creation of web content and as participants in harnessing insights for product development. Let consumer generated content develop your unique brand story.

Communicating your unique value proposition clearly, concisely, and consistently across all marketing communications channels will enable you to build strategic awareness. Strategic awareness occurs when not only do your customers recognize your brand, but they also understand the distinctive qualities that make it better than the competition. Strategic awareness occurs when you have differentiated your brand in the mind of your market.

"An image is not simply a trademark, a design, a slogan or an easily remembered picture. It is a studiously crafted personality profile of an individual, institution, corporation, product or service."

Daniel J. Boorstin

All components of a brand must work together to create a differentiated personality for the brand that heightens awareness while building preference. Such strategic awareness will allow the brand to enjoy greater loyalty from your market while commanding a price premium with better margins.

The ability of a brand to stand out in the marketplace will enhance its chance of standing out in the mind. We live in an over-communicated world where each of us is bombarded with hundreds of branding, advertising and editorial messages daily. If your brand looks like every other brand, it isn't likely to be noticed.

Travelator Commentator

If you've been on the travelator at Bank tube station, you can't have failed to notice Grant Thornton's first international advertising campaign. Based around the insight that 'big decisions follow you around,' the ads feature people in a range of scenarios outside the office, wrestling with tough business dilemmas.

These thought leadership ads are all headed with 'big questions.' It gets pretty interesting when you answer these dilemmas with some Firebrand thinking:

Half the board says now, half the board say wait. Which is the riskiest option?

Everyone says that we are living in interesting times and most will sit there and watch their competitors to see 'what shakes out.' The biggest risk lies in doing nothing allowing your competitors to take the lead. These are opportunistic times - don't wait to differentiate your brand. Take action by finding your unique core essence now and build your brand from there.

Expanding abroad is attractive. How do we make it happen?

Look for market gaps. Create a consistent unique value proposition that can be refined for the needs of each local market.

We've missed our target two years in a row. What should I do if we miss it again?

Put marketing metrics in place. Look at where you are spending your marketing budget and what is most effec-tive. Stop spending money on areas that are not delivering Return on Investment and use that free budget to test one new marketing method that you have never tried before every month.

We have to reduce costs. What are the options this time?

Creating an integrated marketing campaign that builds over time will save the continual re-invention (and significant costs) necessitated by disconnected, one-off tactical campaigns. A consistent design style will not only increase the recognition of your brand, it will lead to production economies.

What We Can All Learn from Meerkat Marketing

An aristocratic furry creature in a velvet smoking jacket stands on a stool in front of the fire in a baronial hall and introduces himself as Aleksandr, founder of comparethemeerkat.com. He is frustrated that people keep coming to his website looking for cheaper car insurance, instead of going to comparethemarket.com!

Let's have a look at a few results. The campaign achieved all of its twelve-month objectives in just 9 weeks. The brand is now number one in spontaneous awareness and consideration. Quote volumes have increased by over 83%. Its cost per visit has been reduced by 73%.

Today, Aleksandr has more than 480,000 fans on Facebook and almost 19,000 followers on Twitter. The comparethemeerkat.com website does actually allow visitors to compare meerkats and has had more than 5.6 million hits since its inception. Comparethemarket.com is now one of the most visited insurance websites in the UK.

We're talking about a market that by its very nature is a commodity – an online financial and utility services aggregator. Comparethemarket.com also had less of an advantage than most. Take the name to start with - it is unwieldy and unmemorable. Its identity was similar to its nearest (bigger spending) competitor, GoCompare. Every competitor was boasting the same key features and benefits. So, what can we learn from Meerkat Marketing?

Focusing on a key word

The only thing that distinguished them was the word 'market.' Focusing on a key word would create their own space between them and their competition.

Creating a brand personality

The leap forward came in not only creating a character but also being clear what type of character they didn't want. They were seeking something that would engage on an emotional level, with all due respect to Michael Winner!

Gaining a lower cost of market entry

Google charges less if people search by brand name, they charge more if they search for something generic. The interesting part of the campaign for me is that it was based partially on the fact that 'meerkat' had a cost per click of 5 pence compared to £5 for the keyword 'market.' Driving traffic to an engaging and entertaining site became a far more cost effective exercise.

Thinking about Search Engine Optimization (SEO)
From an SEO point of view, CompareTheMeerkat is faring incredibly well. The two-way links with the main CompareTheMarket site, together with viral linking from blogs, Facebook, Twitter and YouTube are a powerful combination in the eyes of Google.

Getting involved in the conversation

B2B firms are now starting to think about how they can interact with social media channels.

However, marketers looking to use social media really must become part of social media, not sit outside it. Make a list of online influencers and note the forums in which they are prominent. Join us in checking out what's going on at LinkedIn, Twitter, YouTube, trade forums and blogs etc. Listen actively to how and where you and your brand can engage in conversations and start to plan your social media strategy now.

As the now famous meerkat would say, "Simples!"

Flame Chapter Challenge

In maintaining our flame, we have:

1. Developed key messages and designs that are distinctive, memorable and break through the marketplace clutter.

2. Brainstormed ideas for an evocative brand name and a distinctive corporate identity that maps to the core brand essence in a way that resonates with our target audience.

3. Constructed a brand positioning statement that all customer-facing employees understand and can communicate (a shared, realizable vision as to how the brand will act on its insight, articulated in the form of a practical 'elevator pitch,' including the following elements: target audience, core essence, brand pillars and value proposition).

4. Crafted a series of compelling anecdotal brand stories that fire the imaginations of our customers.

5. Established a list of proof points (facts, figures, testimonials, editorial endorsements) at our fingertips that endorse our key differentiators and demonstrate our competitive advantage.

Step 4 – Glow

"I would rather be a superb meteor, every atom of me in magnificent glow, than a sleepy and permanent planet."

Jack London

Don't Let Your Brand Go Dark

"Anybody who retrenches because of the recession has really got his head in the sand," said John Vanderzee, of the Ford Motor Company, way back in 1991. "You can't not spend."

To increase spending on marketing at this time may seem counter-intuitive, but this is exactly what businesses should be doing right now. Brands with sustained marketing expenditure will create strong competitive advantage by stealing share of voice.

Four ingredients need to be in place for this to happen:

Character – create a leadership positioning based on the core essence of your brand and become the authority in your market.

Culture – foster entrepreneurialism to develop plans, pilot new marketing approaches and roll out successes.

Capital – commit the resources and budget you need to make your plans a reality.

Calendar – put deadlines and milestones against every element of your programme and monitor and measure progress.

In this market, too many senior executives have been watching and waiting on 'what will shake out from the downturn.' So much time is spent agonizing about what they shouldn't do; their greatest danger is substituting 'action' with 'analysis.'

Organizations can get away with this in a boom economy. They can't get away with it now. The antidote to the recession is a commitment to action.

No matter how many ideas you have swirling around, not one of them is worth a penny to you until you actually take action on it. This is the time to choose five new initiatives and test, test, test.

It can be argued that marketing in a downturn is an "opportunity to gain market share at the expense of weaker businesses that choose, or are forced, to cut marketing expenditure," as Peter Field observes in Market Leader magazine. I echo this completely. I've seen the organizations that have cut their budgets struggle to compete in the upturn cycle last time around, while the players who maintained a market presence have since flourished. What I have found particularly interesting was the analysis of the extensive Millward Brown database on the impacts of budget cutting.

The article concludes: "Its data shows a strong correlation between market share and the level of 'bonding' – an aggregate measure of multiple brand–consumer relationship metrics. The clear implication being that if budget cutting results in a decline in 'bonding,' then market share can be expected to decline. Crucially, further data demonstrates that two key constituent brand relationship metrics – brand usage and brand image – suffered considerably (13% and 6% declines respectively) when brands 'went dark' (i.e. ceased to spend on communications) for a period of six months or more. More broadly, 60% of brands 'going dark' see decline in at least one key relationship metric after just six months."

In the past year, I have seen evidence first-hand that suggests that brands that cut their budget relative to competitors are at greater risk of share loss. It's time to shine out in the media blackout.

I read a great quote from Seth Godin. It said: "Professional service marketing is certainly among the safest I've seen. Because it appears to take no risks, it's actually quite risky."

Since safe marketing approaches are, by definition, quite so unremarkable and consequently go unnoticed, these are the ones that put your marketing investment at the highest risk. Ironically, if you want to be truly risk-averse and protect the future of your business and your brand, it's time to stop being quite so 'safe' and identify how you can stand out.

Whilst it has often been argued by academics that niche brands may often achieve high differentiation but low levels of relevance amongst the general population, they have missed the point that they have very high levels of relevance amongst their target segment.

Don't let your audience 'tune-out.'

Product clutter – too many choices and too many product features, resulting in customer confusion.

Message clutter - too many messages, leading to a battle for awareness and the fear of creating adverse disruption.

Media clutter – too many media channels, making it far harder to reach the customer, without diluting marketing spend.

As Jeff Longhurst, Managing Director of Crédit Agricole Commercial Finance, said to me recently in an interview,

"The walls of so many organizations are littered with framed vision statements that mean little to the people who deliver the services and deal with the clients. It was important to us to create a statement that is simple, actionable, achievable and measurable."

The Financial Brand (US) has had some tough things to say about differentiation in financial services markets.

"Human beings are hard-wired to notice things that stand out. There are only a few basic principles that drive all successful brands. You must be able to consistently deliver something relevant to consumers that is different from what your competitors provide. And hopefully, your strategy isn't something your competitors can easily copy. The more your brand meets these criteria, the more successful you will be. But of all the components fueling a strong brand, the most critical is differentiation."

We would go further to say that differentiation is the fundamental purpose of marketing. Controversial perhaps - I believe, incontrovertible.

To create a Firebrand, there must be a view as to how customer needs are changing (insight), what the new opportunities may be (imagination), what these opportunities could look and feel like (illumination) and how the organization should adapt to realize them (implementation).

The techniques of branding have been kept secret for many years because they provided a competitive advantage to those companies that used them.

The difference is usually not 'what you do' but 'who you are' and 'how you do your business differently.'

"It's ain't what you do, it's the way that you do it – that's what gets results!"

Bananarama

From a customer's perspective, a Firebrand is:

1. Relevant - matches our customers' needs, wants and expectations.

2. Remarkable - makes our customers take notice of us and tell other people about us.

3. Reputational - makes our customers feel good, giving them a sense of esteem.

4. Real - matters to our customers creating an emotional bond with our brand and our business.

Getting the 'Glow-How'

"Reputation is only a candle, of wavering and uncertain flame, and easily blown out, but it is the light by which the world looks for and finds merit."

James Russell Lowell

I've just been scanning the agenda on the train to the CBI Conference Centre. All the great and the good will be there and I have some tough things to say about how brands will pull them through and the importance of cherishing clients.

Cherish. It's a word that's not used very much in today's society. It's far more than just having an appreciation for a person or an object. While appreciation is important, it's about caring enough to want to nurture, protect, promote and sustain it - even cling to it. Think of the word 'cherish' and it conjures up the idea of 'unconditional love.' After all, your brand is - or should be - your baby. Whatever label you choose to place on the current climate, it's clear that there are macroeconomic forces at work that are placing new pressures on your business. There are normally three knee-jerk reactions that are applied during times such as these: command and control, paralysis by analysis and retrenchment. Not terms you would associate with cherishing your brand.

Nurture

Clients are feeling more vulnerable than ever and they are more likely to stick with what they know and trust and take fewer risks. Focus on retention - remember why you took your clients on in the first place. Show them you still want them. Don't assume a return to normal - the longer and deeper the recession, the more likely clients will adjust their attitudes and behaviors permanently. Re-evaluate your insights by conducting a client survey and be alive to changing mindsets.

Protect

The goal of marketing during a recession is generally to protect market share at a minimum and ideally to expand it, positioning the brand to perform well post-recession. "We have a philosophy and a strategy," P&G chief A.G. Lafley once told *The Wall Street Journal.* "When times are tough, you build share."

Promote

There's still a lot less noise – and a lot more opportunity. Invest in marketing and you are guaranteed a greater share of voice. Re-evaluate media channels, messages - and everything else. The volume of direct mail has reduced dramatically, so use it. Get your online strategy delivering. Heighten the level of creative and disruptive thinking – hire it in and make your messages 'top of mind.'

Sustain

Don't wait for permission from The *FT* or *The Economist* to declare that the recession is over. Like us, I hope you've made a conscious decision not to participate. Get ahead of the crowd - plan your post-recession strategy now. Don't be one of those companies that just didn't see the changes. Focus on sectors where pent-up demand is going to be unleashed once the economy turns the corner. Don't lose momentum in your marketing – you may never get it back.

Leading with Lovemarks

During meltdowns, the role of emotion is heightened. The tougher it gets, the stronger emotional bonds become. This is a time for love – big unconditional love. As Kevin Roberts, CEO of Saatchi and Saatchi, says, "Brands are built on respect. True lovemarks (which create unreasonable client loyalty) are created out of love and respect." Lovemarks are about relationships, not transactions.

Mastercard 'Priceless' campaign

"What we found was that people buy things because of how those things make them feel… So the idea is that the item allows you to get to some other place in your life that makes you feel good."

Trust – The Currency of Ideas

I have spoken at two conferences recently, the first being the 'Reputation in Financial Services Summit' and the second, 'A Key Person of Influence.' In both forums, authenticity and trust were placed at center stage.

Look up the word 'trust' in the Oxford Dictionary and it states its meaning as 'acceptance of the truth of a statement without evidence or investigation.'

If you look at the front of a £10 note, you'll find the phrase 'I Promise' and on a dollar bill, 'In God We Trust.' The whole of our financial system is based on trust and the delivery of promises. As Robert Phillips, UK CEO of Edelman, said: "Trust is an entry which does not appear on a bank's balance sheet. As an important asset, perhaps it should."

According to the 10th annual Trust Barometer, published at the World Economic Forum in Davos, for the first time, 'trust' (72 percent) and 'transparent and honest business practices' (64 percent) are seen as the most important drivers of corporate reputation in the UK and globally.

Furthermore, an independent survey 'In Banks We Trust?' launched to a financial marketing panel this year, reveals that 58% of financiers feel that corporate communications is key to improving the reputation of the sector.

Roger Steare (corporate philosopher and visiting professor of organizational ethics at Cass Business School, City University, London) visited our specialist supplier group at FIDES recently. He addressed the issue of the triple bottom line consisting of 'People, Planet and Profit.'

"Current accounting standards are another part of the problem. These are only capable of accurately describing 20% to 25% of the full economic value of any enterprise. The alternative of triple bottom line accounting standards is beginning to address this issue, but we are still left with a massive void - our failure to measure the value of human relationships, with all stakeholders, that are the core fundamentals of all human activity."

Creating 'Flambassadors'

"Trust yourself. Create the kind of self that you will be happy to live with all your life. Make the most of yourself by fanning the tiny, inner sparks of possibility into flames of achievement."

Golda Meir

Employer branding

In order to live the brand it is essential that employees feel good about it, and get up each morning full of enthusiasm for their jobs, and feeling the company really cares about them and their careers. This ethos needs to be cultivated as carefully as the consumer brand, and is known as employer branding. A company's employer brand starts with the behavior and actions of the bosses, and is reflected in all areas of company culture. A strong employer brand also allows the company to attract and retain the best staff, and positively impacts on the brand as a whole with all stakeholders.

Living the brand has everything to do with authenticity, clarity and differentiation. The core essence of your brand must be rooted in, reflect and strengthen the culture of your organization before it can ever become a reality to your customers. To engage with your clients, you first need to engage with your internal stakeholders – your employees.

Here are six steps you can take now in your brand's quest for 'internal life:'

- Harvest the experience and expertise of your employees (your internal stakeholders) at an early stage to develop unique value propositions (UVPs) that relate directly to the core essence of your brand.

- Run a workshop for each functional area to identify specific actions that they propose to take to support the practical delivery of these UVPs.

- Then, bring the cross-functional teams together to share their ideas and publish the results as a brand blueprint.

- Run a brainstorming session to create your unique brand vocabulary.

- Involve your team in redrafting all of the standard customer-facing letters and documents to reflect this.

- Create 'boiler plate' wording that everyone can use when asked, "Send me something on your business."

James M. McCormick, president of First Manhattan Consulting Group, has a marketing team that has commissioned thousands of 'mystery shops' and interviews with front-line employees at retail banks. During their visits, his researchers always ask bank employees a simple question: "As a customer, why should I choose your bank over the competition?" Two-thirds of the time, McCormick noted, the employees have no answer to that question; they either say nothing or, in his words, "make something up on the fly."

It is absolutely imperative that senior marketers make differentiation their number one priority. This is the time to workshop, educate, train and mentor front line employees to be able to explain simply and convincingly what makes their organization different from, and superior to, the competition.

A brand is shaped by every encounter with the customer. It is therefore vital that people within the organization live the brand. Although this is important for the entire organization, it is especially important at the customer interface. The sales and marketing team must not only understand the brand, they must care about it too. They must appreciate that everything they say and do significantly effects perceptions of the brand.

Your Brand Vision

Brand vision defines the brand: what it is and where it's going. It needs to set out the brand values, which permeate through all areas of the business, and drive all its activities. It is the personality of the business, which underpins everything.

Why, then, are there so many bland, undifferentiated statements which could apply to any of a number of businesses?

A lack of differentiation is the most critical issue for the financial services sector right now. It is no coincidence that an inspection of the vision statements and customer charters of so many institutions reveals an undifferentiated, uninspiring approach to defining themselves and why they matter to people – so much so, that you might wish to describe the situation as 'the bland leading the bland.'

Be different

Typical of the formulaic corporate offerings are: "Our vision is to make XYZ bank the best financial services organization in the UK." Countless organizations in the UK share statements like this. All you have to do is swap the brand names around and no one would even notice. The '*Simply the Best*' approach should remain with Tina Turner, perhaps to be reprised occasionally at the start of under card boxing matches.

Be specific

Two financiers aim to be regarded as the most admired in their chosen category!

"To be the UK's most admired financial services business."

"To be the most admired retail bank in the world."

Am I alone in finding the wish to be admired expressed in a vision statement, however well intended it may have been, rather cloying in its desire to be noble? What is the impact your business intends to have on your customers or on the world? Is it similar to anyone else? If so, you need to Light Your Firebrand™.

Be bold

"Our ambition is to become one of the handful of universal banks leading the global financial services industry."

With this statement, this financier hasn't attempted to take the lead or to become 'the' anything. Since when has becoming 'one of the handful of organizations' in your particular field ever been considered an ambition?

Be memorable

In my view, HSBC's distilled vision statement, "We are the world's local bank," does everything right.

It fulfils all of the criteria of being different, specific, bold and memorable. When I read that vision, expressed as a strapline, I find myself filling in the blanks – making the bank's offering personal in a way that makes an emotional connection. There is a sense of its strong global presence and perspective. The bank belongs to the world and by implication, the people of the world. They are local and, therefore, closer, implying that they care for their customers and (re-enforced by advertising) that they are an integrated organization that can help businesses expand internationally. It tells me that they not only know where they are, they know where they are going as a business and a brand and that fills me with confidence.

Be distinctive. Encourage us to draw pictures in our minds so that we may have co-ownership of your vision.

Be inspirational

The following five values represent what The Bank of America believe in as individuals and as a team, and how they aspire to interact with their customers, their shareholders, their communities and one another. I really like the first of these particularly:

Doing the Right Thing:

We have the responsibility to do the right thing for our customers, shareholders, communities and one another.

Trusting and Teamwork:

We succeed together, taking collective responsibility for our customers' satisfaction.

Inclusive Meritocracy:

We care about one another, value one another's differences, focus on results and strive to help all associates reach their full potential.

Winning:

We have a passion for achieving results and winning – for our customers, our shareholders, our communities and one another.

Leadership:

We will be decisive leaders at every level, communicating our vision and taking action to help build a better future.

Write your core values

Don't see writing your core values as a dull, corporate exercise to be filed away, never to be looked at again. Be creative and inspirational; produce values which permeate through everything your company does, so that being the best becomes a reality, not a vague ambition.

Living your values

Positioning is about taking a stand, about standing out. It's about having your own agenda and being a leader of your segment of the market rather than being molded by it. Every time a client, prospect or business introducer has a contact with your brand online, offline or in person, your core brand essence and distinctive personality must come across. An original, unique, clear and succinct statement of what you stand for.

Is 'surprising' or 'unexpected' one of your organization's key brand attributes?

How many of your clients would say that your brand is 'delightful?'

ABN AMRO offers its preferred banking clients access to a special lounge that the bank has built within Amsterdam's Schiphol Airport. It's part of a move towards greater customer engagement that has prompted the bank to add 'Surprising. Unexpected. Delightful. Helpful. Innovative. Relevant,' attributes to its brand.

Personally, I like the first two attributes, provided that the customer experience is positive!

Connected by Ambition

With Crédit Agricole Commercial Finance, 'ambition' unites the business and its stakeholders. Its brand pillars are stated here in the form of supporting values to achieving the brand promise or core essence, "Connected by ambition:"

"At Crédit Agricole Commercial Finance, we structure and deliver bespoke invoice discounting, asset based lending and invoice factoring services in order to turn our clients' business ambitions into achievement.

Our core values, cohesion, openness, accountability and entrepreneurship, provide depth and focus to all of our relationships.

Crédit Agricole Commercial Finance has placed these four values at the heart of our business. They are a critical element of our corporate strategy and we apply them to every business situation for the commercial advantage of all our clients.

Cohesion

We bring you the best of both worlds: The experience and local knowledge of a nationwide team, combined with the financial strength, presence and resources of one of the largest banks in the world.

Openness

We maintain the highest standards of integrity, honesty and transparency, with an emphasis on listening, mutual trust and open-mindedness.

Accountability

We hold ourselves totally accountable in delivering our promises and accept responsibility in everything that we do.

Entrepreneurship

We are committed to working in partnership with our clients, supporting their ambitions and sharing with them the excitement, intensity and commitment they bring to their businesses."

The Brand Iceberg

The key to branding success is to embody the brand itself in ALL words and actions. They also recognize that the relationship with the brand deepens as everyone becomes involved - moving from awareness to understanding as the essence of the brand comes alive through creating a clear, differentiated client experience. Ultimately, brand equity is the sum of all the hearts and minds of every single person that comes into contact with your company.

In the best-managed brands, the entire workforce accepts the brand's values. The employees have a relationship with their brand that is the counterpart of the intended client relationships. This recognition that brands now serve as much more than just an identity system is illustrated by the concept of the Brand Iceberg. Like an iceberg, only a small proportion of the brand's mass and power is visible, the rest is intangible and hidden. But effective brand management requires attention to the hidden brand elements as much as to the visible ones.

External

Name

Brand identity

Brand experience

Marketing collateral

Advertising

Public relations

Referral

Products & services

Internal

Brand values management - control

Structure

Internal communications

Business process

Training

Quality

Staff motivation

Knowledge management

Recruitment policies

HR policies & processes

Technology

Don't get first impressions wrong

While we're at this point, let me just let off steam about a particular bugbear of mine. *Think about the message being given by your reception.* I went into an office the other day, great building and location, enthusiastic greeting from the staff, but the company was really let down by the general plethora of boxes, dirty coffee mugs, even the receptionist's spare shoes! First impressions are vital.

Given this, why is it that so many companies continue to have the most junior, most poorly trained, lowest paid employee on reception? Or, worse still, a poorly briefed temp?

What would happen to the client experience if the whole corporate structure was turned on its head and you had one of your most senior, highest paid employees to fulfill the role of 'First Impressions Director'? Someone who lives and breathes the core essence of the brand, who makes an accomplished elevator pitch, who knows the unique value propositions of the business.

Simply calling your receptionist may reveal some of the challenges customers face and inform your rebranding strategy. Take the time to navigate your own website, buy your products and return something. Better yet, ask a friend or family member to do so and learn from their experiences.

Your brand must have a credibility internally. If employees who live the brand day-to-day don't believe, the target audience won't either.

Genius service

We all know them. Just say the magic word, 'Apple,' and off they go. Any excuse to preach the virtues of the infinitely superior Mac over the PC. True fanatics, they love Macs and all things Apple. And they are probably Apple's most effective sales force. I'm one of those fans – even when things go wrong.

Last week, something did go very wrong. I must have gone through the KeyNote Triangle, somewhere near Clapham Junction. I was unable to launch this amazing software on my Mac Air – just before I was due to make an important presentation. Truly *Up the Junction,* I did the only thing that anyone would do under the circumstances and took the tube to Oxford Circus and ran like the wind to the excellent Apple Store Genius Bar. Trained at Apple headquarters, Geniuses have extensive knowledge of Apple products and are able to answer any technical questions and troubleshoot issues.

The Genius in question, Ambrose, couldn't have done more to help and fixed the issue within minutes at no cost. He was a genuine brand ambassador for Apple. The level of service I received made me think about what the we can learn from the customer experience at the Apple Store:

- Access – immediate support on a walk-in basis, without having a prior reservation (not always possible but gratefully received!)

- Approachable – friendly, accessible and professional

- Ability – highly trained staff with first rate technical knowledge

- Authority – empowered to make decisions without deferring to higher authority

- Articulate – answering customer queries and explaining technical issues without jargon

- Action – rapid, effective issue resolution and use of initiative to make it happen

For experiences like these, Apple will rightly be rewarded by:

- Higher visitor numbers

- Increased sales

- Superb public image

- Satisfied customers

- Greater job satisfaction for staff

- Repeat business and customer loyalty

Apple comes across as the company that cares, that will do the right thing by customers. It's an example of the brand proposition delivered – which in turn enabled us to deliver our presentation.

Ron Johnson, the Senior Vice President for Retail at Apple, has often referred to the Genius Bar as the 'heart and soul of our stores.' To me that sums up what customer engagement is all about and, today it is more important than ever. Apple knows it. Ambrose knows it. Most businesses could learn a great deal from it.

A connection with a brand only becomes real when it's on an emotional level. Emotional connection is driven through experience of the brand leading to familiarity, confidence and trust at the level of engagement.

Pleasure and pain!

Try to become much easier to deal with than your competitors. Separating the 'pleasure' from the 'pain' is one smooth step towards enhanced customer engagement.

Disney sums it up perfectly, "When there is both pain and pleasure associated with your service, work extremely hard to separate them by time and geography."

Your prospects want the products and services you are offering. After all, your solutions provide a series of benefits they want and need. More often than not, they solve a serious problem that affords your prospect 'pain relief', if not yielding them exciting new opportunities. Deep joy!

To neglect employing a call to action or to avoid collecting basic contact data on your web site are both missed opportunities - even marketing crimes. But do you really need that lengthy sign up page? Wouldn't it be better to collect a detailed level of data after you have made contact and built both trust and permission with your prospect? If the pain of completing a long, highly detailed form is involved before your prospects even feel they know you, they may just end their contact with you right then and there.

Many companies have moved towards online quote strategies and these create a new obstacle. These organizations may look technically savvy but the reality is that they have effectively delivered the pain (cost) before the prospect has had any meaningful contact or exposure to the brand. The prospect has all of the information they need to compare you with your competitors, with no contact, no opportunity to engage with the brand or the brand ambassadors. And no contact means no contract.

Start the dialogue by asking your prospect for less. You'll gain so much more.

Robert Blanchard, former P&G executive said in *Parting Essay* -

> *"People have character...so do brands. A person's character flows from his/her integrity: the ability to deliver under pressure, the willingness to do what is right rather than what is expedient.*
> *You judge a person's character by his/her past performance and the way he/she thinks and acts in both good times, and especially bad. The same are true of brands."*

Applied physics

Just like the three laws that govern all of physics, there are a set of fundamental truths about how customer experience operates. And here they are, the 6 laws of customer experience:

1) Every interaction creates a personal reaction.

2) People are instinctively self-centered.

3) Customer familiarity breeds alignment.

4) Unengaged employees don't create engaged customers.

5) Employees do what is measured, incentivized, and celebrated.

6) You can't fake it.

Many organizations seem to have forgotten that it is seven to ten times more costly to attract new customers than to retain existing ones. All the new, fresh and exciting offers are designed to appeal to and attract new clients, not reward existing customers. OK, clients feel vulnerable right now and this is manifested in terms of significant inertia. That can change frighteningly fast.

Never forget that today and in the future, the customer will be even more self-empowered. Napoleon Bonaparte said it all, "I can no longer obey; I have tasted command, and I cannot give it up!" When we emerge from recession, clients will wish to exercise that choice like never before.

Newton's First Law: Every object in a state of uniform motion tends to remain in that state of motion unless an external force is applied to it.

You must apply force to get momentum. Sales will stay in a constant state unless and until you apply your marketing effort. Standing still is NOT an option when you want your organization to move forward.

Newton's Second Law: The relationship between an object's mass m, its acceleration a, and the applied force F is $F = ma$.

A budget applied regularly month on month is more effective in combination than a large budget applied once or twice.

Newton's Third Law: For every action there is an equal and opposite reaction.

One off advertising or a one-shot email may get you awareness but no response – so don't do it (at least not unless it is in tactical support of a wider PR campaign). Be aware of this important law and allow yourself to build your relationships and trust with your readers over time.

Beware celebrity endorsements

In a statement, Tiger Woods says that he regrets his recent string of 'transgressions' and speaks of not being true to his values.

What impact do his personal values have on the brand values of those companies who have aligned themselves to him via sponsorship? Why is celebrity endorsement a problem in terms of Light your Firebrand™? The relationship of brands to high profile, celebrity would seem to be perfectly aligned and the ads are, after all, in the main well executed creatively.

There are four reasons why it is important to beware of celebrity endorsements:

- You are buying into an image over which you have no control. (What if the celebrity you choose is involved in a scandal?)

- You are introducing two brands into the equation, which may potentially confuse the target audience.

- You are potentially diluting your own brand's power.

- You have a relationship with a celebrity who has other more powerful and relevant brand linkages. (In Tiger's case, Nike - which does matter if it eclipses other sponsor deals in scale, reach and presence)

Firing Up Your Tribe

"When you discover your mission, you will feel its demand. It will fill you with enthusiasm and a burning desire to get to work on it."

W. Clement Stone

A great deal is spoken today in marketing circles about creating communities. A customer's sense of community, linked directly to your brand, re-enforces top of mind status and leads to a deeper level of engagement. For a community to be adopted by customers, a need to connect with other customers in the context of the brand's consumption is vital.

Such interactions with fellow brand users include:

Sharing - user group forums, wikis, seminars and events where knowledge, data and technical information can be stored and shared easily are very powerful ways of developing dialogue within communities.

Validation - members of brand communities often display a strong desire to be validated or accepted by fellow members, gaining esteem through association. Typically, this is focused on a strongly differentiated attribute and a sense of what is 'cool,' whether this is engendered by technology or style.

Personality - members of the Apple computer brand community feel a strong sense of expressing their personality by espousing all things Apple and by so doing (vocally and passionately) rejecting the market leader Microsoft.

Esotericism - this refers to the doctrines or practices of esoteric knowledge, that which is specialized or advanced in nature, available only to a narrow circle of 'enlightened,' 'initiated,' or highly educated people.

Some theorists on branding suggest that the community-building aspects of a business are what characterize good branding. Branding experts in this camp place greater emphasis on embedding the brand ideology into the culture of the organization first, and then allowing that culture to diffuse to customers and the public. Increasing community for the brand, then, becomes the key component of successful branding.

"If one reviews the emergence of innovative brands such as Crocs, Ben and Jerry's, Facebook and others, these were begun and manifested by creating community," said Drew Stevens, an adjunct instructor of marketing at West Virginia University and president of Stevens Consulting Group. "Even thought leaders today such as [Seth] Godin are very good at building brand this way. The emergence of Marketing 3.0 will require brands to think about how to continually increase community for the brand."

You've got to wow your customers at every possible opportunity. Your employees are the life-blood of the business and are crucial to its success. You have to start internally to get employees engaged in the brand and cultivate the culture that will encourage them to behave in ways that will affirm the brand.

By understanding the essence of the company's brand and being empowered through a set of shared values and standards to deliver on that essence, your employees will instinctively know how to act on those values. Employees need a clear focus on what the brand stands for – the values, the style, the personality and the point of differentiation. When employees know the company and understand the brand then, and only then, can they communicate it to the customer.

Running With Torches

"The hero is the one who kindles a great light in the world, who sets up blazing torches in the dark streets of life for men to see by."

Felix Adler

Trust is a word used a great deal in business. Like reputation, trust is something that is hard earned and easily lost. Building trust is an essential part of feeling an emotional connection with a brand and this comes from positive shared experiences with the brand over time.

A greater balance between functional and emotional brand values may serve to stimulate value creation and sustainable differential advantage. The ability to communicate on a more intimate level helps break through the constant noise that consumers are bombarded with each and every day.

Ethical values and beliefs engage with clients on a deeper level than functional attributes, as The Body Shop has shown. On a totally different motivational level, aspirational positioning to the 'privileged few' can elicit desire for specific luxury products e.g. the esteem conferred by owning, say, a Lexus LF-A.

A cohesive visual vocabulary is a powerful means of creating an emotional connection. This may consist of a carefully chosen mix of your corporate identity, corporate colors, fonts, an icon, character or images designed to endorse your brand personality and tell your unique story, speeding up the brand recognition building process.

Despite an ever-expanding array of marketing platforms, consumers still place their highest levels of trust in other consumers, according to the recent global Nielsen Internet survey. Conducted twice-a-year among 26,486 internet users in 47 markets from Europe, Asia Pacific, the Americas and the Middle East, Nielsen most recently surveyed consumers on their attitudes toward thirteen types of advertising from conventional newspaper and television ads to branded web sites and consumer-generated content. 78% of respondents said they trusted the recommendation of other consumers above all else.

It follows that video testimonials are powerful ways of highlighting a positive brand experience in a real way. The warmth and sincerity of delivery as well as the emotions expressed will build the credibility of your messaging through the power of 'social proof.'

"An organization can only 'walk the talk' when its managers deliberately shape its internal reality to align with its brand promise...(the brand's) values must be internalized by the organization, shaping its instinctive attitudes, behaviors, priorities, etc."

Alan Mitchell, *Out of the Shadows*

Start with your own people. Involve them, listen to them and inspire them. Then it's far easier to emotionally connect with customers. Above all, be authentic, genuine and truthful.

Engagement goes beyond reach and frequency to measure people's real feelings about brands. It starts with their own brand relationship and continues as they extend that relationship to other customers. As a customer's participation with a brand deepens from site use and purchases (involvement and interaction) to affinity and championing (intimacy and influence), measuring and acting on engagement becomes more critical to understanding customers' intentions. The four parts of engagement build on each other to make a holistic picture.

The reality is that your existing customers make the most powerful brand evangelists, for testimonials, co-creation of web content and as participants in harnessing insights for product development. Let consumer generated content develop your unique brand story and help you Light Your Firebrand™.

However, what does this mean for today's marketers?

First, it focuses on the belief that continued customer engagement is always an ultimate brand objective. Secondly, it gives us clear criteria by which our success in attaining the optimum state of customer engagement may be measured:

Involvement - *comprises customer participation at various brand touch points.*

Interaction - *concerns the actions taken by a customer at those brand touch points.*

Intimacy - *consists of the affection that a customer holds for a brand.*

Influence - *is the probability of a customer recommending your brand.*

Immersion - *takes into account the depth and breadth of customer experience (which I believe is of primary importance as a practical barrier to exit).*

Integrity - *which is concerned with the quality, and authenticity of that engagement.*

The golden rules are: first be found, and then be found interesting.

Interruption marketing no longer works. People are more adept than ever at being able to filter you out. They ignore banner ads, they skim through commercials on Sky Plus and TIVO, and they click to another site in seconds if they don't see what they're looking for. Pull marketing, on the other hand, is about engaging your prospects and clients in a way that attracts them towards you.

The loyalty factor

There are ten major business factors that directly influence the loyalty and commitment of customers:

Values - core attributes and beliefs that resonate with your clients.

Positioning - unique value propositions (attributes not found within your competitors).

Satisfaction - delighting your clients with superior service.

Offering - relevant products and services that fulfill specific needs.

Location - locale can be a strong determining factor for high touch services.

Inertia - client / market apathy can affect loyalty – however this is fragile and can be reversed given the right conditions.

Difficulty of Switch - if there are too many hoops to jump through or hurdles to leap.

Involvement - the greater the degree of interaction and collaboration the harder it is for a competitor to break into and break up the client relationship.

Demographics - synergies such as population characteristics and alignment to a service can prove highly effective.

Share of wallet - the percentage (share) of a customer's expenses (of wallet) for a product or service that goes to the firm selling the product or service.

"Google actually relies on our users to help with our marketing. We have a very high percentage of our users who often tell others about our search engine."

Sergey Brin, Founder of Google

"A brand that captures your mind gains behavior. A brand that captures your heart gains commitment."

Scott Talgo

The 4Rs highlight how a Firebrand can gain heartshare:

Remarkable - the brand is unique, making an impact on the client.

Reputational - the brand is admirable and the association builds customer esteem.

Relevant - the brand stands for something important and pertinent in the eyes of the customer - providing a solution to a problem or creating an opportunity.

Real - the brand connects with the customer on multiple levels across several senses.

Mindshare is accomplished through defining a shared core brand essence and relevant unique value propositions. Heartshare can only be achieved when the values and beliefs that support that core essence permeate the company at every level from hiring criteria, training to organizational culture.

Ultimately, values cannot be imposed; they have to be inherent within the business. Purpose cannot be manufactured; it must be felt like a cause. And if that sounds hard, so it should. Because it is.

Gaining referrals

1   From day one, clients should be made aware that referrals (and testimonials) are a key part of your business. After all, that is how they may well have been introduced to you, so the concept is unlikely to be completely alien to them.

2   The market for your referrals is characterized by inertia and latent demand. If you're gaining referrals at the moment without asking for

them, you'll double or triple the number you get when you ask. Ask in person, ask by mail and email, and ask on the phone. Ask – and keep asking.

3   Remember that clients are not just doing you a favor by giving you a referral. We actually ENJOY giving referrals. Don't you like recommending a great movie you've seen to a family member or friend? Your clients will actually get pleasure from giving the people they know the same good service experience they've had. This is one of the reasons that asking for referrals works better than many companies think.

4   Thank your clients when they give you referrals. Send them a letter or call them.

5   Reward your customers for giving you a referral. Either with a gift, or something of value from your business or, if appropriate, with cash. The better the gift, the more likely they are to give you more referrals.

6   Many firms are poor at harvesting and measuring client referrals and don't have professionally integrated mechanisms or processes in place to do so. If this applies to you, have a specialist marketing agency create a formal referral system where you regularly and consistently 'market' client referrals. Promote your business referral process with a carefully planned sequence of emails, direct mail, phone calls and meetings.

Channel relationships

Companies often ask me how prospective channel relationships can be developed to become powerful business-driving partnerships.

Powerful partnerships - the 4Cs

I have developed the 4Cs model for the purpose of assessing partnerships and this takes into account the following criteria:

Congruence - first, we examine the closeness of fit to the client's existing introducer base - size, structure, geography and service / product gaps etc.

Contacts - then we look at the network base (the introducers' client base) and identify how closely this matches with the type of business we are looking for.

Culture - we assess the beliefs and cultural fit of the leading players.

Commitment - and we look at the level of commitment they have to the partnership - shared project marketing budgets, direct mail, PR and news bulletins, other joint promotions to accelerate business development.

Consider connecting by:

Industry or sector (direct or partner channel association with a market).

Wants and desires (synergy with the same end-game in mind).

Beliefs and culture (cause related association with like-minded individuals and groups).

Complementary services (project teams, JVs, closing skills gaps, bundling, white label).

Information (vital data for key information seekers).

Geography (proximity, location, ethnicity).

Distribution (similar routes – physical and online, gaps).

Marketplace (buyers and sellers).

Technology (mash ups, shared platforms).

Outside interests (shared experiences).

The Firebrand marketer

I believe that there are five key ways that Firebrand marketers can gain the respect that their role deserves, in order to be recognized as true growth and value drivers, not cost centers.

1. They must be bold visionaries, leading the strategic agenda of the business. They possess the ability to face any level of competition, thrive during economic fluctuations, and grow into additional markets.

2. In owning the growth agenda, they must set specific, measurable, business-focused outcomes - what gets measured gets done.

3. Marketing plans must be based on cross-functional delivery of the strategic business plan across the entire organization, so that everyone is engaged in the process of value creation.

4. The language used by Firebrand marketers should be the language of the boardroom, not of the marketing text-book. Talk about profit - not promotion, margin - not marketing communications.

5. Accountability in delivering top and bottom line results is the fifth and most vital imperative.

Tim Ward, finance director of the FTSE Group and former head of marketing at the London Stock Exchange has some clear tips for marketers on winning friends and influencing people, not least amongst our finance director colleagues. Here are 4Ps that will lead to a closer alignment with the FD / CFO:

Positive

"A good relationship with the finance director will ensure that everyone is clear on marketing's contribution and how it fits into the business model."

Proactive

"Budget time can be one big confrontation. But if the conversation has been constructive well in advance and the evidence is properly laid out, it should be obvious to both sides what's needed."

Process

"We're not looking for a complete financial analysis, just something that can be measured over time."

Profit-oriented

"Marketing is like any other project when it comes to fighting for budget. It should be clear how any given activity generates benefits for the business. This means concrete revenue, not things that might lead to it, such as brand building."

Building a true Firebrand is summed up perfectly by Michael Eisner, who says: "A brand is a living entity - and it is enriched or undermined cumulatively over time, the product of a thousand small gestures."

That said, Firebrand marketers deliver more than stewardship, more than mere direction, they fuel the fire, keep it roaring.

It's almost time to take the Test of Fire...

Glow Chapter Challenge

Following this chapter, we will have:

1. Educated our clients to understand how our brand promise is unique and how it is distinct from our competitors' propositions.

2. Allowed our clients to participate and interact with our brand.

3. Generated an affinity and an emotional connection with our customers and our brand.

4. Encouraged our clients to give written and verbal testimonials about us.

5. Built up a following of influencers who actively recommend our brand, products and services to others by word of mouth.

The Test of Fire

"We're going to be okay, aren't we Papa?"
"Yes. We are."
"And nothing bad is going to happen to us."
"That's right."
"Because we're carrying the fire."
"Yes. Because we're carrying the fire."

Cormac McCarthy - The Road

Taking the Firebrand Challenge

You can do more with a magnifying glass than look closer; it's almost time to start your fire. But, before you do, take a look at the following statements and see how you score..

Please use this section as a quick checkpoint against the key concepts in this book, so you can see how far you've come on your Light Your Firebrand™ journey.

> To what extent do you agree or disagree with the statements below?
>
> Strongly agree (10 Points)
>
> Agree (5 Points)
>
> Disagree (0 Points)
>
> Through the Light Your Firebrand™ process, we have:
>
> 1. Gained a clear understanding of why repositioning and brand revitalization are imperatives for our business.
>
> 2. Established a deeper understanding and appreciation of our customers and their needs.
>
> 3. Identified the threats and opportunities facing our business.
>
> 4. Focused on developing specific strategies to meet these challenges, maximizing our strengths and minimizing / eliminating our weaknesses.
>
> 5. Mapped out how we differ from our top five competitors at each stage of the marketing mix.

6. Identified key attributes for which we can potentially command a leadership position.

7. Distilled our brand down to one key word that we want to 'own' in our customers' minds – our core essence.

8. Engineered / re-engineered our unique value proposition around our core essence to provide meaning for our customers.

9. Identified clearly defined brand pillars (the guiding insights and qualities that support the essence of our brand).

10. Created a brand vocabulary for all employees that maps directly to the core essence of our brand.

11. Developed key messages and designs that are distinctive, memorable and break through the marketplace clutter.

12. Brainstormed ideas for an evocative brand name and a distinctive corporate identity that maps to the core brand essence in a way that resonates with our target audience.

13. Constructed a brand positioning statement that all customer-facing employees understand and can communicate (a shared, realizable vision as to how the brand will act on its insight, articulated in the form of a practical 'elevator pitch,' including the following elements: target audience, core essence, brand pillars and value proposition).

14. Crafted a series of compelling anecdotal brand stories that fire the imaginations of our customers.

15. Established a list of proof points (facts, figures, testimonials, editorial endorsements) at our fingertips that endorse our key differentiators and demonstrate our competitive advantage.

16. Educated our clients to understand how our brand promise is unique and how it is distinct from our competitors' propositions.

17. Allowed our clients to participate and interact with our brand.

18. Generated an affinity and an emotional connection with our customers and our brand.

19. Encouraged our clients to give written and verbal testimonials about us.

20. Built up a following of influencers who actively recommend our brand, products and services to others by word of mouth.

How did you get on?

See how your brand scores in the Light Your Firebrand™ Challenge:

A 150 - 200 Congratulations – You have the strong potential needed to Light Your Firebrand™.

B 100 – 145 You are well on your way to Light Your Firebrand™.

C 50 - 95 Some elements of successful branding are in place, but a greater focus on planned brand development is needed for you to Light Your Firebrand™.

D 0 - 45 You still have some way to go before you are able to Light Your Firebrand™.

Brand Measurement

The 4Rs Test

Ultimately, a brand must stand up to being measured by the 4Rs test. For a brand to fulfill its promise, the 4Rs must be adopted at every level from corporate strategy through to engagement with the customer.

The 4Rs can be expanded upon as follows:

Remarkable

The starting point for all brands is awareness. To become differentiated, a company must identify the features of its brand that make it truly unique and distinctive compared to competitor or substitute offerings. They must look for what sets the brand apart. Failure to stand out from the rest leads to price competition and low margins in a desperate and harmful attempt to attract customers.

Reputational

This refers to how well regarded the brand is. The reputation of your brand is an important factor in attracting customers. The more esteem they have for the brand the less risky they will consider the purchase.

Relevant

Although differentiation is critical, it is not the whole story. Differentiated features must also be relevant to customers, or they are of no value. A brand becomes relevant by offering features that customers consider important. These features meet a base level of expectations and send the message that the brand is credible. They might include good service, competitive pricing, or other positive attributes. Because customers expect these base features they become me-too. Such offerings are not distinctive, and as a result are not unique from competitors.

Real

A connection with a brand only becomes real when it's on an emotional level. Emotional connection is driven through experience of the brand leading to familiarity, confidence and trust at the level of engagement. This is an indicator of a high potential for loyalty and referral the value of which should not be underestimated.

Applying the 4Rs

You can apply the 4Rs to a simple grid system, enabling you to discover more about the dynamics of your business and how it is currently positioned. A Firebrand stands up to being measured by the 4Rs test. These principles cascade from a strategic level right the way through to engagement with the customer.

You can have a highly differentiated brand on which you can credibly deliver and people still might not care. You have to strike a chord. The best way to accomplish this is by (1) listening to a (2) narrowly-focused audience so that you can (3) understand their unique needs.

In each of the following examples, the concept of having a remarkable brand is played against the other three attributes, as shown below.

Remarkable / Relevant

The first example concerns a shopping trip I made to Carnaby Street. I bought four suits, yet I didn't intend to buy four when I set out.

Things get a lot more interesting when you start to compare style and fit, by plotting 'remarkable' with 'relevant'. In this example, the 4Rs look like:

- Relevant (fit)

- Remarkable (style)

- Reputational (esteem)

- Real (experience)

High Relevant, High Remarkable

Haute Couture - good fit, looks stunning, dress to impress.

Low Relevant, High Remarkable

Fashion Nightmare - looks great on a hanger but that's where it ends.

High Relevant, Low Remarkable

Work Wear - functional, fits OK but you wouldn't feel great wearing it on a big night out.

Low Relevant, Low Remarkable

The Hanger - poor fit, dull color, doesn't make it to the changing room.

Remarkable / Relevant

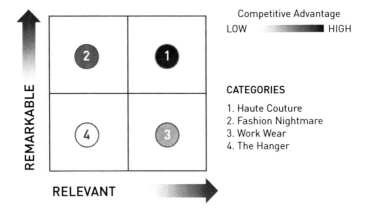

Remarkable / Reputational

In this example, using a soccer analogy, reputational is played against remarkable:

High Reputational, High Remarkable

Star Striker - in form premiership star, scoring for fun as the pundits say.

Low Reputational, High Remarkable

Substitute – spends more time on the bench than on the pitch. Can make a difference as an impact player - however, is unproven, may be inconsistent and lack stamina or experience to see through an entire game at top level, maybe only stands out in weaker company - possibly the star of the reserve team.

High Reputational, Low Remarkable

Failed Transfer - expensive purchase but failing to do it on the pitch, not cutting it in premier league company.

Low Reputational, Low Remarkable

Pub Team Player - makes up the numbers in the local pub team, unlikely to get scouted for his dubious talent.

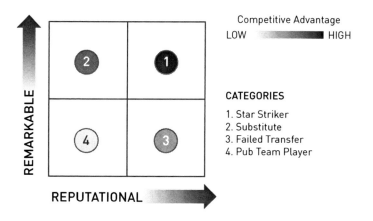

Competitive Advantage
LOW   HIGH

CATEGORIES

1. Star Striker
2. Substitute
3. Failed Transfer
4. Pub Team Player

Remarkable / Real

In this example, I have sought out the bright lights of the nightclub for inspiration. Here, 'remarkable' jostles with 'real' on the dance floor.

High Real, High Remarkable

Love at First Sight - the glance across a crowded room, time stands still, dreams are fulfilled in the upper right quadrant.

Low Real, High Remarkable

Pretty Vacant - stunningly attractive and memorable for all that but an emotional void.

High Real, Low Remarkable

The Wallflower - pleasant enough, may get a dance where there is limited choice, convenient at the time, but ultimately a low involvement decision.

Low Real, Low Remarkable

Can't Dance, Don't Ask Me - doesn't get noticed or make any concerted attempt to engage at any level.

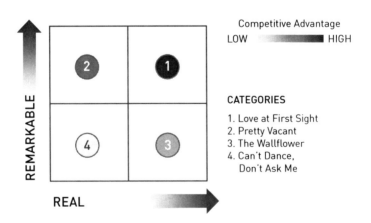

Competitive Advantage
LOW ▬▬▬▬▬ HIGH

REMARKABLE

REAL

CATEGORIES
1. Love at First Sight
2. Pretty Vacant
3. The Wallflower
4. Can't Dance,
   Don't Ask Me

The 4Rs in action

Here are comments made by Annabel Pritchard, brand manager at Deloitte, highlighting why the firm's emphasis on using its 11,000 staff to ensure its brand proposition is delivered resulted in its recognition as Best Brand in B2B Marketing magazine.

Remarkable

"The rebrand was very visual for the first couple of years, but it has moved on. We're still responsible for its visual aspects, but more significantly, we're focused on getting people involved and understanding what makes Deloitte different."

"We're not the only professional services company that did outdoor advertising, but we thought about it carefully, and we probably spent more. The aim was to be different and bold. Advertising on the Imax is something usually associated with consumer brands, but Waterloo is also a prime location for commuters. At another location we took four billboards and put nothing on them. That was brave. It's not what people expect from us. We want to be part of the Big Four, but also different."

Reputational

"Our CEO describes our brand as 'classic with a contemporary twist.' Blue is a trusted corporate color, but we want to be seen as forward-looking and contemporary. The green dot is designed to communicate trust and the insight we bring to our clients. We want to be seen as quietly confident, not arrogant."

Relevant

"We have 50 (brand champions) across the organization, generally in management. Their role is to help understand what is right and to consult with the business on this."

Real

"Branding in professional services is very different from FMCG (Fast Moving Consumer Goods). Our people are our brand. Their behavior delivers and reinforces it. You can set expectations through sponsorship and advertising, but it's the people who make the difference."

"This kind of engagement and passion," she says, "is the 'Holy Grail' of professional services marketing."

The SPACE Model™

"They believed in space exploration. They knew the risks, but they believed in what they were doing. They showed us that the fire of the human spirit is insatiable."

Charles Camarda

Market research needs to abandon its pretensions that the customer has predictive powers as a guide to the future.

Experienced researchers recognize that many customers are, in fact, future-blind and apathetic until stimulated into taking action and being shown the new opportunities being promoted. At the same time, however, social media is empowering customers to get more involved in the generation of ideas and collaborative product development.

Using the 'brand-past' as a guide to future action may help the customer recognize our messaging in a tracking study, but the findings will only condemn us to merely repeat the past. Market research may re-enforce what we already know, it may even give us 'color' in terms of consumer attitudes and perceptions but it won't shift markets. Only the adoption of new thinking can do that.

That's why we have developed a proprietary differential marketing model. One that is practical and proven to transform the way in which companies do business at a deeper level – we call it the SPACE Model™.

We are now using this Model to rank and measure the perceptions of clients, partners, directors and staff in a highly visual form of gap analysis. It can even be applied to specific products or used at a granular campaign level.

The SPACE Model™ not only provides a brand snapshot. It is predictive over time, since there is a direct correlation between a lessening in differentiation and the accelerated rate of a brand's decline. The good news is that the opposite is also true in terms of adoption and ROI.

Data is collected about the brand using a carefully structured survey, which focuses on these five key areas:

- **S** Strategy
- **P** Positioning
- **A** Architecture
- **C** Communication
- **E** Engagement

In this example, I have used the survey data to plot the 4Rs on a radar chart against the SPACE attributes using survey data. You can identify at a glance where issues and opportunities exist.

As you can see, this business has clearly focused exclusively on tactical communications, without the balance or true alignment we would expect from a brand that have been developed through the Light Your Firebrand™ process.

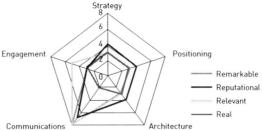

Your unstoppable Firebrand

In a world of relentless change, in which customers have infinite choices and unprecedented power, it's almost impossible to compete without having a compelling brand. Creating one, however, demands passion, insight, imagination and a proven process that delivers breakthrough results.

Branding is a continuous process – you can't let your fire die down to its burning embers and you have to be ever-vigilant in monitoring the flame. In existing markets, you have to fan the flames continually with the oxygen of creativity to keep your messages fresh and relevant. In new markets, you may have to set a number of small fires before the kindling starts to blaze. Whatever your strategic goals, don't neglect your Firebrand - strive to keep the 4Rs in perfect balance.

The process is there to support you at every stage until you have reconnected with your burning ambition.

Revisit and repeat the exercises again as often as you need. Involve your team. Inspire your customers. Blaze your trail with your unstoppable Firebrand.

Additional Elements

"The desire, enthusiasm and fires are there, and this selection has only intensified all those elements."

Lawrence Dallaglio

Bonus Features

Maslow under the microscope

Many years ago, I was speaking with a corporate psychologist at The Bank of New York about Maslow's hierarchy of needs. They rolled out the classic pyramid, starting at the base with the so-called **deficiency needs** - physiological, safety, social, and esteem – and finishing at the apex with **self-actualization needs**.

I made the great mistake of 'sharing' my view that in a relatively affluent society and particularly in B2B markets, most so-called deficiency needs are being met to a greater or lesser extent and that to resonate with our clients and introducers we need to flip the pyramid on its head. The white-knuckle ride through my cerebral cortex that followed is confidential!

However, I am now going to leak the most contentious contents of my file exclusively for you!

Scaling Maslow's pyramid his way, with **physiological needs**, having been met, we progress to satisfying **safety needs**, which may be manifested by demand for credit protection, confidential facilities, audit trails, robust corporate governance, etc. **Social needs** recognize that we all act as connectors, not just directors. Connections may be achieved through inter-company alliances, group working or at an individual level. Web 2.0 examples that satisfy these needs are social networking environments, blogs, wikis and forums - virtual worlds where like-minded people can connect based on affinity and where marketers can share their 'cause' and engage at a deeper level.

Everyone in a management position has **esteem needs** to some degree, where it is manifested as the requirement for recognition or a greater sense of contribution. Increasingly, experiential marketing involves customer involvement in collaborative product decisions, having greater control over how services are delivered or distributed. The ultimate empowerment for the customer is for them to rewrite your brand story continually.

Self-actualisation needs are the most advanced and this is the place where we find what I call Mindshare and Heartshare.

Mindshare is what Maslow would relate to as the **cognitive** level of self-actualisation. He believed that humans have the need to increase their intelligence and thereby chase knowledge. Cognitive need is the expression of the natural human need to learn, explore, discover and create to get a better understanding of the world around them. Harness this desire for knowledge in the pathways to gaining enquiry. Involve the customer with transactional tracking capability. Educate them with tailor-made Amazon-like accuracy - 'people who bought this item, also bought...'

Heartshare combines **transcendence needs** (giving back, enriching others or championing a cause) and **aesthetic needs** (personality, values, beliefs and behaviors).

According to Maslow, the tendencies of self-actualizing people (entrepreneurs) are as follows:

1. **Awareness**

   Efficient perception of reality, freshness of appreciation, peak experiences, ethical awareness.

2. **Honesty**

   Philosophical, sense of humor, social interest, deep interpersonal relationships, democratic character structure.

3. **Freedom**

   Need for solitude, autonomous, independent, creativity, originality, spontaneous.

4. **Trust**

   Problem / solution centric, acceptance of self, others, nature, identity with humanity.

It's a vision of the modern consumer, of the early adopter, that sought-after, dreamed-of viral referral source that makes just about everything happen for your brand. Find them and your brand will fly.

The 6 Ts

There are 6 Ts of continuous improvement that will deliver us to that place where we can even start to compete in this new landscape: targeting, testing, tracking, tempting, triggers and testimonials.

Targeting

Have you captured the addresses for every single contact, whether direct or channel influencer? If you haven't assembled the data for your entire universe mail or e-mail-ready for your next marketing campaigns, you're not even in the game. In addition to targeted marketing in clearly focused trade magazines, this is the time for one-to-one marketing using email and digital print.

Testing

Controlled, real-time pilots enable you to gain an immediate view of the competitive environment and will help you predict the likely success of rolling out an integrated program for a particular product or service.

Tracking

Email marketing gives you the ability to track communications and specific content links in detail - and in real time. You'll see precisely who opened the email, whether they re-visited it and what products and services are of greatest interest to them. You can, therefore, tailor your branded content specifically to meet their information needs.

Tempting

Be different! Find a way to offer something unique that cannot be found anywhere else. Your most important, unique, and least easy-to-copy point of differentiation should be the unique value proposition for your brand and serve as the basis for your pitch. Align your offer strategy to your core brand essence and promote it powerfully.

Triggers

Many financial brands are now looking to real-time data streams such as trigger data to inform the marketing process. The 'what if?' possibilities are endless and the benefits of customer satisfaction, loyalty, up-sell, cross-sell and product development are far reaching for the entire community. Early technology adopters have everything to gain.

Testimonials

Many prospective customers will want to see evidence of satisfaction from your existing clients, particularly from the same sector and regarding the specific products they are looking to buy from you. Much underplayed, industry-specific client testimonials underpin your benefits statements and build your reputation.

It seems odd to think that a recession might well prove to be the catalyst to make marketing more effective. In fact, I believe that it will result in a new era of best practice.

For those who keep their heads below the parapet in marketing terms, or worse still, risk burying their heads in the sand right now, the future will be all too crushingly certain. This is not the time for invisibility but rather a time when companies should work even smarter to stand out.

The 4 Cs

The ways in which potential customers respond to marketing communications has been subjected to rigorous scrutiny and refined over decades. E.K. Strong's AIDA principle, 'attention, interest, desire, action,' is perhaps the best known of these, still quoted by many marketers, but in contemporary terms, it is a very simplistic model.

I have no doubt that the more complex business environment we face today requires a new three dimensional behavioural model based on the effective awareness, control and management of the three states defined below:

Cognitive (thinking)

What is the meaning of the information?

Recognition - to sense the information.

Reasoning - to think about the information in order to find results or draw conclusions.

Reflection - to reconsider or reaffirm thought processes.

Response - to start to form conclusions, subject to connective processes.

Connective (feeling)

How do I feel about this information?

Empathy - to identify with the issues raised.

Emotion - to have strong feelings about these issues.

Esteem - to value the proposed solution, benefits and brand attributes.

Energy - to make an effort, desire to make contact.

Conative (doing)

How will I act on these thoughts and feelings?

Fact Find - to probe, information gather.

Formulation - to develop ideas and intentions.

Finalize - to refine, distil, crystallize.

Follow Through - implement decision - either purchase or referral, depending on the nature of the client or channel relationship.

The order of these states is defined by the degree of involvement required in order to make a purchasing decision. B2B markets tend to work with high-involvement decision-making that supports the 'natural' order of cognitive (thinking), connective (feeling) and conative (doing) dimensions.

Generally, the prospective client will be seeking assurance about the company and the product in order to feel the level of trust to complete a purchasing decision. In the first instance, the purchaser is driven by the need to gather information (cognitive state), so they can feel assured (connective state), before they are comfortable to complete (conative state) the transaction.

This is particularly characteristic of complex, high-risk, infrequent transactions.

The fashion industry operates in a similar dimension, yet with the dominant emotional bias, the order and emphasis changes to create a connective - cognitive - conative decision-making pathway.

Low-purchasing decisions may be conative - cognitive - connective in the case of daily purchases of staple consumer goods or conative - connective - cognitive in the case of an impulse purchase.

The Conative Campaign - Knowledge to Act

I noticed a series of striking text-based ads from Thomson Reuters on the tube. The key messages support their 'Knowledge to Act' campaign.

Each of the ads reveals a different aspect of the business and it struck me immediately that the nature of the proposition is fundamentally conative.

The first creative execution is headed, "The end of think. The beginning of know," which is a theme echoed in the line "It's no time for 'think.'" This culminates in the dependable proposition, "Knowledge that businesses and professionals rely on worldwide."

Here, the proposition is played out by emphasizing the inherent dynamism of the process in response to Board pressure, driving towards a decision to act instantly, eliminating or subjugating both cognitive and connective dimensions:

The end of think. The beginning of know.

"Markets are watching. Your board is waiting. It's no time for 'think.' Enter Thomson Reuters, the world's leading source of intelligent information. Thousands of industry experts filtering vast databases of information with the most intuitive applications. Checkpoint. Westlaw. Reuters News. It's knowledge that businesses and professionals rely on worldwide. Thomson Reuters - Knowledge to Act."

The second ad in the series serves to highlight the difference between feeling and knowing. Although friendship is mentioned, the decision-making process taps into gut instinct and experience, rather than the world of emotion and feelings. The proposition for this advertisement centers on trust:

Introducing a better gut instinct.

"Trust your instincts. Trust your experience. Trust the world's leading source of intelligent information, business insight and knowledge to act, for businesses and professionals; information mined, analyzed and filtered by the smartest software anywhere. Thousands of industry experts. Friend to your gut. Thomson Reuters - Knowledge to Act."

The third ad execution is creating empathy based on peer knowledge and experience, resulting in robust insight and knowledge that drives action:

Insight from people who don't just get what you do. They do what you do.

"Taxation, finance, accounting, healthcare, law; thousands of experienced specialists working for you 24/7. Add the most intelligent insight-generating software in the world and you get the world's leading source of intelligent information, business insight and knowledge to act; for businesses and professionals. Thomson Reuters - Knowledge to Act."

Like the ad before it, the fourth and final ad maps out the target audience as businesses and professionals. This ad sharpens the focus still further by utilizing peer-to-peer or aspirational positioning, citing the Fortune 500 amongst its clients. We are told that they 'help uncover decisions', suggesting a process or discovery that leads to action:

Decision in a haystack.

"Plea bargain? 'Launch Invest?' We're the world's leading source of intelligent information, business insight and knowledge to act, for businesses and professionals (including the entire Fortune 500). With insight mined from reams of data by experts who do what you do, we help uncover decisions. Thomson Reuters - Knowledge to Act."

Firebrand Jargon Buster

A client asked me recently about our Light Your Firebrand™ Workshops and it made me think that it would be helpful to set out some definitions at the end of this book. Here is a jargon buster style glossary of phrases that we use within our workshops at Strand Financial:

Awareness The percentage of population or target market that is aware of a given brand or company - either spontaneously or when prompted.

Brand The cumulative impression of a company's image, attributes, tangible and intangible, positioning, logo and experience. It defines what the company stands for in the marketplace.

Brand Architecture How an organization structures its brand portfolio. There are three main types: monolithic, where the corporate name is used on all products; endorsed, where all sub-brands are endorsed by the corporate brand and freestanding, where the corporate brand operates merely as a holding company, and each product is individually branded for its market.

Brand Associations The feelings, beliefs and knowledge that consumers (customers) have about brands.

Brand Commitment The degree to which a customer is committed to a given brand in that they are likely to re-purchase.

Brand Development Model A model for defining a brand essence, core positioning and attributes - in support of corporate strategy.

Brand Earnings The share of a brand-owning business's cash flow that can be attributed to the brand alone.

Brand Equity The value of the brand to its owners as a corporate asset.

Brand Essence / Core Essence The distillation of a brand's intrinsic and differentiating aspects into a succinct and enduring core concept. The heart and soul of the brand, which transcends market and cultural variances.

Brand Experience The means by which a brand is created in the mind of a stakeholder by consistent interactions at key 'touchpoints'.

Brand Expressions How the brand is expressed (visually, experientially) at the points of consumer contact.

Brand Extension Leveraging the values of the brand to take the brand into new markets/sectors.

Brand Harmonization Ensuring all brand elements are harmonized in support of the Brand essence and positioning.

Brand Identity The outward symbolic expression of the brand, including its name and visual appearance.

Brand Licensing The leasing by a Brand owner of the use of a brand to another company. Usually a licensing fee or royalty rate will be agreed for the use of the brand.

Brand Management The deliberate management of all the tangible and intangible aspects of the brand to create the desired brand experience among consumers, consistent with the core brand positioning.

Brand Personality The attribution of human personality traits (seriousness, warmth, imagination, etc.) to a brand as a way to achieve differentiation.

Brand Pillars The guiding insights that support the essence of the brand.

Brand Revitalization A major overhaul of a brand, starting with its essence, positioning, attributes, values and brand architecture.

Brand Strategy A plan for the systematic development of a brand to enable it to meet its agreed objectives. The brand strategy should influence the total operation of a business to ensure consistent brand behaviors and brand experiences.

Brand Tone How the brand communicates and tells its story to its target audience.

Brand Values The code by which the brand lives (the corporate DNA). The Brand values act as a benchmark to measure behaviors and performance.

Brand Valuation The process of identifying and measuring the economic benefit - brand value - that derives from brand ownership.

Brand Vision A view of the role, scope and goals of the brand moving forward.

Brand Vocabulary / Brand Thesaurus The vocabulary used by the brand to give a unified 'language' to the team.

Co-Branding The use of two or more brand names in support of a product, service or venture.

Corporate Design The guidelines for visual identity of a corporation (its imagery and tone of voice).

Corporate Identity The standards for visual identity of a corporation (its mark or logo, signage, design parameters).

Corporate Brand (Parent or Master Brand) The central brand that manifests the corporation's identity and positioning. It also acts as the endorser to one or more sub-brands within a range.

Customer (or Brand) Touch points All those points where a customer comes in contact with the brand.

Differentiation Making a brand stand out in the market by positioning its tangible and intangible assets.

Endorsement Use of the corporate brand to support the credibility of an allied or sub-brand.

Online Branding (Digital Branding) All branding activities in an online environment.

Perceptual Mapping Analyzing a brand against its competitors in terms of various criteria (i.e. brand strength, awareness, associations). An important step in developing a distinctive brand positioning.

Positioning The distinctive position that a brand adopts in its competitive environment to ensure that individuals in its target market can tell the brand apart from others.

Rebrand When a brand owner revisits the brand with the purpose of updating or revising based on internal or external circumstances. Rebranding is often necessary after an M&A or if the brand has outgrown its identity/marketplace.

Repositioning Communications activities to give an existing product a new position in customers' minds and so expanding or otherwise altering its potential market.

Service Brand A product consisting predominantly of intangible values. "A service is something that you can buy and sell, but not drop on your foot." *The Economist*

Share of Mind There are many definitions of share of mind. At its most precise, share of mind measures how often consumers think about a particular brand as a percentage of all the times they think about all the brands in its category.

Share of Voice The media spending of a particular brand when compared to others in its category.

Sub-Brand A product or service brand that has its own name and visual identity to differentiate it from the parent brand.

Target Market The market segment or group of customers that a company has decided to serve, and at which it consequently aims its marketing activities.

Trademark Any sign capable of being represented graphically that is capable of distinguishing goods or services of one undertaking from those of another undertaking.

Top-of-Mind Present in the uppermost level of consciousness; the manufacturer or brand that people in market surveys name first when asked to list products in a specific category.

Choosing an Agency

A common folly committed by companies with their eye on the bottom line is not to get professional marketing help early enough. (I would say that, wouldn't I?) Yet skilful professional advice actually increases profits by maximizing marketing opportunities and preventing costly mistakes, which might even jeopardize the business.

Choosing the right agency to communicate your business edge is a tough call, particularly if you haven't had to do it before or if your existing agency hasn't delivered. Consider the following points:

Does the agency understand your objectives?

Is the marketing agency a true sector specialist? Have the directors worked client side as well as agency side? If the answer to both of these questions is 'No', walk away – they lack the experience and knowledge of your sector. If they are specialists, the marketing agency's understanding of your business objectives will be reflected in their response. If they do not provide an insightful analysis of the business issues and challenge the brief intelligently, look elsewhere.

Can the agency differentiate your business?

Is the agency capable of producing big ideas that will help you to Light Your Firebrand™? Have they got to the core essence of your brand? Can they position your business effectively?

Is the agency producing results for its existing clients?

What are the clients saying about their agency? Have they given positive testimonials regarding the quality of the work?

Does the agency have the right credentials?

What kinds of brands is the agency working for right now? What are the skill-sets and levels of experience of the people? Do they have clients that 'fit' with your company's profile?

Will you be dealing with the directors of the agency?

Be sure that you meet the people who will be working on your account. Will your account be delegated to a lightweight? Or will you be dealing with experienced people at the top of their game?

Will your account be important to the agency?

It is important that your account is seen as being significant and special on every level, considering diverse elements such as willingness to gain a close working knowledge about your business and your brand.

Does the agency realize that advertising is not always the solution?

"Advertising is the solution, now what's the problem?" is a widely held view held by traditional agencies. A progressive marketing agency must demonstrate that it has a full working knowledge of the most appropriate options.

Is the agency capable of integrating offline and online media?

Integrated marketing is concerned with a holistic, solutions-based approach that consistently delivers results on an ongoing basis. Today, you need an agency that spans both of these media arenas.

Does the agency offer high-level strategy and creativity?

Within any campaign, strategy and creativity must be applied with the perfect weight. Ensure the agency can deliver on both.

Is the agency's motivation to take your business to the next level or to win awards?

A client's business success beats the pursuit of CLIOs every time. Make sure the agency is intent on adding value for your business, rather than trophies to its cabinet.

Briefing an Agency

The right briefing to your agency will make all the difference to producing the best creative results. This ten-point guide sets out the secrets of successful briefing.

1. **Background**. What's the big picture? What does your business do? What's happening in the market?

2. **Objective**. What is the objective of the marketing activity - enquiry generation, profile raising? What is the anticipated result? What effect should the communication have? What do you want the target audience to think, to feel, to do?

3. **Target Audience**. Who exactly are we talking to? The more precise and detailed the answer, the better. Demographics, psychographics, age, gender and geography will all paint an insightful picture of the people you want to communicate with.

4. **What do we want to say?** What is the core essence of your brand? What are your company's UVPs? What is the single-minded proposition for this specific communication? Avoid generalities – these only result in ambiguous communications.

5. **What do we need?** What is the desired format, structure, size, scope and description of the marketing activity or collateral? What is the 'call to action' or response mechanism?

How will the communication be distributed to the target audience?

6. **What are the mandatory elements?** Here's where you put the other details. What logos, contact names, telephone numbers, codes / references must be included?

7. **When do we need it?** A realistic date for delivery is essential. This will vary depending on the nature of the activity or communication, the delivery address and the number of people being communicated to. Always give your agency ample time for idea generation.

8. **How many do we need?** Frequently forgotten in the initial stages of the briefing process, the quantity is a very important factor in terms of determining the marketing communications budget.

9. **What is the budget?** Do you have an appropriate budget allocated for this level of activity? Can you give the agency a 'ball park guide' since even this can be helpful? It is important that the budget is realistic; too little can compromise the success of the campaign and make your business look bad.

10. **What is the approval process?** Who signs off the brief / estimate? What is their availability? Include the name, telephone number, address and email address of the person (people) commissioning the work and with the responsibility for signing it off.

Agency Briefing Template

		Project:	
Issued By:		Version/ Date:	

BACKGROUND

Target Audience

Core Essence

Brand Pillars

UVPs

Elevator Pitch

Proof Points

OBJECTIVES

STRATEGY

DESIRED RESPONSE

SINGLE MINDED PROPOSITION (USP)

CREATIVE STYLE

COPY/TONE OF VOICE

MANDATORY ELEMENTS

RESPONSE MECHANICS

TIMINGS

Trending topics

When it comes to your marketing, put all of your sacred cows out to graze. Eliminate the average. Look outside your immediate markets for inspiration. Focus on a strong, distinctive core brand essence. And above all, be original and authentic. Here are some new 'word constructs' to describe the key trends and predictions:

Disruptiation

(Disruptive Differentiation)

Only disruption will lead to optimum differentiation as companies look to break away from the stranglehold of sameness for survival. Today, it will not be enough to offer a me-too service or share value propositions with your competitors.

Themetics

(Memetic Themes)

Themetics are remarkable ideas, linked to a central strategically developed theme, that are deliberately spread throughout a culture and are absorbed by a receptive community. KPIs should focus on downloads, embeds, forwards, mentions and comments.

Tribalogy

(Tribal Technology)

The creation of passionate groups or tribes around a common interest, market, product or geographic reach will become even more important. The Tribalization of Business study by Deloitte has found that 94% of businesses will continue or increase their investment in social media next year.

Altiances

(Alternative Alliances)

While it makes sense to build partnerships in good times, the rationale for alternative alliances is even more important today. Strategic alliances allow firms to create new bundles of value, increase distribution, expand into new markets, test new approaches, fill market gaps, reduce overhead, leverage resources and share risk.

Vidlocity

(Video Velocity)

A viral video is a video clip that gains widespread popularity through the process of Internet sharing. Vidlocity speeds up and amplifies messages by seeding videos to influential journalists, bloggers, and Twitterati, and spreading content across channels and communities.

Apcceleration

(Application Acceleration)

This is the time when marketers start to get their heads round really useful mobile marketing applications. By that, we are not talking about old-school WAP web sites. It's the right time for marketers to start to make the most of the app revolution and accelerate development.

Entergagement

(Entertaining Engagement)

If content was king in previous years, this year engagement is the key to success. This comes from the recognition amongst marketers that content must in future involve target audiences by entertaining and informing them in fresh and compelling ways.

Stratmetrics

(Strategic Metrics)

Most marketing measurement efforts so often lack strategic input and vision. Marketing analysts are really good at tracking campaign results and even predicting future responses. However, their responsibilities are often to maximize tactical program performance rather than measure the influence of marketing across their firm's strategic goals.

Trustferral

(Trusted Referral)

Word of mouth marketing and client referral tends to be passive, yet has the potential to increase business in multiples and at a superior conversion rate to many other forms of introductory sources.

Medigration

(Media Integration)

Media convergence is a concept in which old and new media intersect: when grassroots and corporate media intertwine in such a way that the balance of power between media producers and media consumers shifts in unpredictable ways. See how integrated marketing techniques can be migrated to a new and shifting landscape. Adapt, adopt, improve.

The 10 Immutable Laws of Innovation

Here are ten points that will help you think even more innovatively about building your Firebrand:

The Law of Intelligence – don't make important brand decisions in a vacuum.

The Law of Interpretation – listen closely to the market when you're treading new ground.

The Law of Impact – be distinctive, bold and original – if you can't lead your existing segment in positioning terms, create a new segment you can lead.

The Law of Invention – invest time in developing or re-inventing your core brand essence, brand pillars and unique value propositions.

The Law of Inspiration – think creatively to differentiate your brand, solve a specific problem or create a specific opportunity.

The Law of Image – focus on maintaining a consistent, coherent image that resonates with your core market.

The Law of Integration – gain organizational commitment at every level.

The Law of Impression – reverse-engineer your brand from the perceptions you wish to create in the prospect's mind.

The Law of Interaction – engage in conversations with customers, encourage a dialogue of ideas.

The Law of Influence – identify how you can gain great testimonials and referrals as a result of your commitment to continued innovation.

Survival of The Fittest

Brands that should rightly come to the fore have a common vision, mission and set of values, which are distinctive and relevant, and which are recognized and understood by all stakeholders. A successful brand will adopt, embed and manifest its values wherever it appears and in whatever form (from its corporate image, marketing collateral and web site to the customer experience received at every touchpoint).

Bail-outs aside, in commercial terms, an ecological system is analogous to a 'free market' of perfect competition. Just as living organisms compete, often with limited resources to survive, so do financial institutions.

Herbert Spencer coined the phrase, "survival of the fittest," in *Principles of Biology,* (1864) to describe Charles Darwin's theory of Natural Selection of living species. It is interesting to note that the concept of Natural Selection is not about the 'survival of the fastest,' 'survival of the strongest,' or even 'survival of the biggest'.

Of course, 'survival of the fittest' in this context doesn't relate to the most highly trained and physically energetic. It means those organisms which are the most suited to their environment and, ultimately, to survival itself.

The three essential components of evolution via natural selection include:

Genetic Diversity: Even members of the same species have characteristics that vary from one individual to the next. Brands must hone individual attributes and a core essence that effectively differentiates them from everyone else in their business environment.

Relative Fitness: In any given environment, some individuals have characteristics that put them at an advantage over individuals who do not possess them. Look for unique value propositions, new attributes and message gaps that your competitors do not own and yet are of high relevance and importance to the customer and to the changing conditions of the environment.

Population Shift: In any given environment, those individuals who have advantageous characteristics will generally be healthier and thrive. Organisms that are not suitably adapted to their environment will either have to move out of the habitat or die out. The current spate of mergers and acquisitions could create a void in the landscape – either by losing competitors or because the new organization is so preoccupied with the integration process that it loses ground. This may allow companies to create their own space and colonize areas left behind. Conversely, strong new organizations can emerge, with more powerful attributes than before and dominate a market. Just as the survival of organisms may be linked to a particular ecological niche, i.e. they are a good fit for their environment, so financial organizations focused on geographical sectors or industry segments can thrive if the conditions are right.

Which brings me to my point. An individual brand with distinctive attributes, perfectly suited to needs of its environment can create market shift. It can only sustain or improve its competitive superiority where it adapts to the demands of its changing environment continually.

On Mergers & Acquisitions

Remember the scene from American Psycho?

> **_Daisy_**: *What do you do?*
>
> **_Patrick Bateman_**: *I'm into... well murders and executions mostly.*
>
> **_Daisy_**: *Do you like it?*
>
> **_Patrick Bateman_**: *It depends. Why?*
>
> **_Daisy_**: *Because most guys I know who work with mergers and acquisitions really don't like it.*

Is the treatment of brands in M&A situations similarly that brutal? In many cases, regrettably, the answer has to be a resounding 'yes.'

Intangibles are starting to play a greater part within the asset mix and brands should in theory become the hot boardroom agenda item for corporate advisers, asset based lenders and company executives alike.

John Stewart, Former CEO, Quaker said, "If this business were split up, I would give you the land and bricks and mortar, and I would take the brands and trademarks and I would fare better than you." It follows that intangibles should form an integral part of corporate responsibility. One of the fundamental objectives of any merger or acquisition should be the intelligent optimization of brand equity, rather than some Darwinian survival of the fittest. Finance directors and marketing directors therefore need to become more proficient at working together pre-merger to assess product brand portfolios and recommend investment / delisting decisions.

Why then are brands treated in such a cavalier fashion, discussed fleetingly after the deal has been structured and potentially lying neglected in the spreadsheet entitled 'cost structures?'

Strategists Joseph Benson and Jack Foley conclude that there are four principal brand strategies for merging brands:

1. Black Hole: only the brand of the acquiring company survives.

2. Harvest: the equity in one brand is extracted until customers transfer their loyalty resulting in the surviving brand commanding a potential price premium.

3. Marriage: both brands seek to create meaningful and relevant differentiation in the minds of the customers.

4. New Beginnings: merging finance companies see that their brands have little or no brand equity, so elect to launch a new brand.

So much of the focus within the financial services industry has been on differentiation at product level in order to drive short-term tactical initiatives in pursuit of targets. There have also been so many mergers and acquisitions within this sector, that there is a real danger that brand differentiation of individual firms is becoming muddied, cloudy and ultimately lost along the way.

Mergers and acquisitions have for too long been a brand battleground where egos win over equity, arguably one of the greatest reasons why so many mergers fail to create shareholder value. I would urge advisers, asset based lenders, CEOs and CFOs to think very carefully about brand stewardship issues during the due diligence process, before it is too late.

FireQuotes

Real Quotes

"It is not slickness, polish, uniqueness, or cleverness that makes a brand a brand. It is truth." Harry Beckwith

"A brand that captures your mind gains behavior. A brand that captures your heart gains commitment." Scott Talgo

"A brand is a living entity - and it is enriched or undermined cumulatively over time, the product of a thousand small gestures." Michael Eisner

Reputational Quotes

"A brand for a company is like a reputation for a person. You earn reputation by trying to do hard things well." Jeff Bezos

"Google actually relies on our users to help with our marketing. We have a very high percentage of our users who often tell others about our search engine." Sergey Brin

"Ordinary people can spread good and bad information about brands faster than marketers." Ray Johnson

Remarkable Quotes

"Something remarkable is worth talking about. Worth noticing. Exceptional. New. Interesting. It's a Purple Cow. Boring stuff is invisible. It's a brown cow. Remarkable marketing is the art of building things worth noticing right into your product or service." Seth Godin

"A lady, sitting next to Raymond Loewy at dinner, struck up a conversation. "Why", she asked "did you put two Xs in Exxon?"

"Why ask?" He asked.

"Because", she said, "I couldn't help noticing?"

"Well", he responded, "that's the answer."
Alan Fletcher

"Marketing and innovation produce results; all the rest are costs. Marketing is the distinguishing, unique function of the business."
Peter Drucker

Relevant Quotes

"Customers must recognize that you stand for something." Howard Schultz

"Marketing is the art of meaningful differentiation." John Lederer

"A brand is a set of differentiating promises that link a product to its customers." Stuart Agres

"To uncover hidden category needs, don't ask 'How can I differentiate my brand from its competition?' but rather ask 'What are the unmet needs that no brand is addressing?'"
Janine Keogh

More Firepower

"Once the fire is lighted under it, there is no limit to the power it can generate."

Winston Churchill

Light Your Firebrand™ Workshop

We understand that branding programs can be extremely difficult to plan, develop and manage internally. Clients come to Strand Branding and Strand Financial for a clearly defined core essence – their distinctive brand promise distilled in the simplest, most single-minded terms. The starting point is a proven, professionally facilitated, highly interactive one-day Light Your Firebrand™ Workshop.

The Light Your Firebrand™ Workshop:
Ignites your purpose, defining the core essence of your brand.

Sparks the imaginations of your management team in a shared, realizable vision.

Illuminates your company's irresistible points of difference.

Creates an elevator pitch that enables your unique value propositions to shine.

Delivers a marketing action plan that will enable your messages to spread like wildfire.

Agenda

Our Light Your Firebrand™ Workshop Agenda is as follows:

- Objectives
- Core Brand Essence Definition
- Brand Pillars Development
- Redefining the Organization
- Value Proposition
- Key Messages
- Brand Promise
- Proof Points
- Elevator Pitch
- Vision Statement
- Brand Vocabulary (Ask the Thesaurus)
- Brand Voice
- Brand Appearance
- Validation
- Marketing Action Plan Brainstorm
- Next Steps

For more information regarding Mike Symes' Workshops, DVDs and Workbooks, visit **www.LightYourFirebrand.com**

Lightning Source UK Ltd.
Milton Keynes UK
10 March 2011
168999UK00001B/29/P